A COMPREHENSIVE ANALYSIS OF THE LAW OF THE OMBUDSMAN

Mohammad Salim Malik, Ph.D
Advocate High Court (Pakistan)

aberdeen university
press services

This book is printed on acid-free paper.

Published by Aberdeen University Press Services.

Printed in the United States of America
ISBN: 978-0-6151-4692-8

This book is printed on 6" x 9", perfect binding, 60# cream interior paper, black and white interior ink, 100# white exterior paper, full-color exterior ink. Prices are subject to change.

Cover Title Designed by Aberdeen University Press Services.

A Comprehensive Analysis of the Law of the Ombudsman
First Edition
Mohammad Salim Malik

"DEDICATED TO ALL THE OMBUDSMEN, THE CUSTODIAN OF THE POOR MEN OF THE SOCIETY"

PREFACE

It is great pleasure for me to write this research topic of ***"A Comprehensive Analysis of the Law of Ombudsman".*** In every society a weak has always suffered at the hand of strong & resourceful. Man is social animal and hence cannot escape impact of the events confronting the society. There is no society where people have not grievances against the governmental machinery. With the lapse of time the society crafts grew complex & demanding the society require redressing their grievances. The only way to redress the grievances of the poor man of very society is to invoke the door of Ombudsman. As the object of establishment of the institutions of the Ombudsman is to eradicate maladministration and grant promptly relief to the aggrieved persons free of cost. Ombudsman law is in the nature of welfare legislation introducing accountability in social administration for achieving good governance, healthy culture and providing clean & friendly atmosphere which may restorate trust of society and confidence of social workers, thereby increasing the ideal social administrative institutions. Ombudsman has to diagnose, investigate, redress and rectify an injustice done to a person through maladministration by functionaries' administration country laws. One of the most effective impacts of an Ombudsman's office, as independent oversight institutions, is to create a feeling of accountability and responsibility in the departments towards the society.

Dispensation of justice at one's doorsteps has been the ideal of human society. The institutions of Ombudsman the world over has been consider a leap forward to achieve this ideal which aims at providing justice to all citizens without getting involve lengthy procedural requirements of the judicial system and also at not cost at all. With the object of protecting the society from the accesses of the concerned departments caused by maladministration, relief has been provided to a large number of complainants directly while thousands of other have benefited from the recommendations equally applicable cases.

I wish to highlight that the performance of the office of Ombudsman, due to its effectiveness and credibility, has created a sense of confidence in the community of poor men of world society, in general there is an institutional arrangements for redressal of the grievances of the poor men of the world society.

I also take this opportunity to highlight the problems faced by the institutions of Ombudsman in Pakistan in the following words:

Non-delegation of the financial and administrative powers to the FTO on the analogy of sister institutions like Wifaqi Mohtasib, Federal Shariat Court, Election Commission of Pakistan, etc. Further, hardship to the taxpayers exists with regard to President's directive of December 10-2001. According to the earlier directive of November 8-2001 of the Honourable President, once a representation is filed by the CBR, status quo had to be maintained by all concerned. The directive referred to above reverse this decision. Now only the recommendations of the FTO are to be kept in abeyance. The result of this change is that while the Department complained against proceeds with impunity with impugned action, the recommendations made by the FTO remain unimplemented. This causes hindrance in the process of justice. Furthermore, office accommodation available for the FTO Headquarters in Islamabad is highly insufficient. The staff members of the FTO's office have been housed at two different places due to non-availability of required space at one place.

I gratefully appreciate the works of the European and other writers on the subject, which helped me to research this topic. I highly thankful the Honourable **Mr. (Ret) Justice Salim Akhtar**

The First Federal Tax Ombudsman of Pakistan, Honorable Mr. (Ret) Justice Munir A. Sheikh The Existing Federal Tax Ombudsman of Pakistan and All other Country's Ombudsmen as well as world wide Ombudsmen who have established tangible literature in the shape of authorities available in various law books of the country and abroad. which actually enable me to research this topic I have dedicated this book to all the Honourable Ombudsmen who are actually the custodian of poor man in this modern society.

CONTENTS

CHAPTER 1

HISTORICAL PERSPECTIVE

Chapter I

Chapter I

1. ***PRE ISLAMIC ERA***

i. The evolutionary process of distribute of justice has taken a chequered track through the ages. For a long period of time, even the norms of justice remained unidentified on the absence of any developed social structure worth the name. However, with the passage of time, due to the growing awareness of people to receive social justice, humane treatment and fair deal the governing privileged could not grasp it back for long. Overthrow and control of the people was slowly but surely giving way to conciliation and peace-making manner. The individual ruler followed by oligarchy condescended to concede certain basic rights of possession and property by devising some organism to deal with social duty, which, hitherto, was grossly undermined.

ii. Recorded history bears witness to misrule in many forms under authoritative oligarchy, autocracy, monarchy and theocracy etc. in history of human civilization. . In the dynastic rule of China and Han, we find an improved system of dealing with complaints and a common citizen could get redress of their grievances against public functionaries by approaching the designated authorities. The Christianity too had taken due care of the under privileged people and its tenets that “blessed weak and poor” served the guideline to the powerful. The people then could protest their grievances to their mentors for necessary help.

2. POST-ISLAMIC ERA

i. In fact Islamic Era is reckoned from immigration to Madian. It is then only the foundation of an Islamic state was laid. A comparatively well-knit system exposé the powerful accountable to the rights and privileges of the meek and weak emerged with its full fame. For the first time in the history of civilization, the income and wealth of the nation was recognized as "Public Property". The prophet Muhammad (P.B.U.H) did not exempt his own self from the

Commandments of GOD. In fact he (S.A.W) was the first to submit him to the Quranic injunctions. Resultantly Islam proclaimed the time-honored principle of equality before law. It is a recorded fact that he (S.A.W) allowed several cases of tort against his person. The prophet of Islam (S.A.W) had thus demolished the centuries old theory of delightful rights of the kings. Even now the countries, which claim to be highly advanced, and civilized count not completely, do away with of the above concept and the maxim that "King can do no wrong" is still held absolute in England.

"Believers are but a single brother hood"

ii. Islam though held equal rights and equal responsibilities of the Muslims irrespective of their country, race, color or language, has also recognized and respected the rights and privileges of the non-Muslims residing in an Islamic state. All rights of a citizen were protected under the law and he was also free to act and live within the limits fixed by the law. None has to trespass the rights of others freedom of expression and liberty of ethics were the corner stones of the Islamic polity.

iii. As reflected from the rights, justice and equity both constituted alarming pillars of an Islamic state. None, Muslim or no Muslim, rich or poor is prevented from protesting against deprivation or injustice and whenever one had lodged the complaint, he got the justice in no time. Even the highest had to explain and justify his act and conduct with the people at large. Holy Quran proclaims.

"Verily Allah loves those who are fair and just"
(Al Hujrat XI-XIV-V)

iv. It is well illustrated in the famous saying of Hazrat Ali (May Allah be pleased with him) That. “A country can survive with “Kuffir’ but it can not survive with Zulm (cruelty)”

The Ombudsman system, strictly speaking, is the sign of what Islam has intended the rulers to follow if the good governance is the definitive idea and aim of any govt.

Chapter I

CHAPTER 2

HISTORICAL BACKGROUND REGARDING CONCEPT AND SCOPE OF ACCOUNTABILITY

Chapter II

Chapter II

HISTORICAL BACKGROUND REGARDING CONCEPT AND SCOPE OF ACCOUNTABILITY

1. The Concept and Historical Feature of Accountability

i. The phrase "Adl" used in Holy Quran is multidimensional since it includes the distinctive between right and wrong. In fact Islam stands for the absolute justice, there by meaning the whatever is done or what is right and correct and hence ultimately in accordance with the commandments of God the almighty. The golden principle of "Adl" (justice) as conceived in the following Hadith if followed in this true spirit can definitely under-write a society free from cruelty and mistreatment.

" None of you will be fully a Momin (a righteous person) till he wishes that for others as he desires for himself and till he loves the mankind for the sake of God" (Al-Hadith)."

ii. Allah Almighty has created Adam and made him the ruler on Earth When Khilafat (Sovereignty) was conferred on him, the significance of "Accountability" was also incontestably established. When Adam faulted, he sought forgiveness and Allah asked him to leave the 'heavenly abode', and wait for guidance on earth from him. Adam's descent to earth was the beginning of the foundation of the state and of the principles as to how the affairs of men shall be controlled by men of course under the supreme command of the creator. Accordingly he was made accountable for his deeds before his creator. From here the concept of "Rule of Law" was evolved.

iii. Dr. Victor Pickle, Australian Ombudsman who was impressed with the concept of accountability in Islam in his paper" The Ombudsman and Administrative Reforms" has traced the history of accountability and good governance as under:

Chapter II

"Institution to investigate complaints can only be seen in the context of public administration; as whole. It goes back to the Holy Quran. In the Koran (Holy Quran) itself the term 'administration' is not used, but in many of its verse the principles of a political and administrative system are expounded. Justice is one of the basic principles of Islamic Ideology. Not only the rulers are responsible for it but the exercise of justice is a task for the whole Muslim society and should be practiced without regard of social status, race, or religious creed. Among Greeks and Romans, on the other hand, sharp distinctions were drawn between different persons and organization in which rights were vested."

iv. The concept of accountability has always been the cardinal feature of Islam. All human beings will be required to render account of each and every moment of their dealings on earth on the 'Day of Judgment'. Accordingly the sources of good public administration are not something discovered in the modern time, which emphasize the scientific approach to the accountability.

v. For the first time in the history of the world, the prophet of Islam (P.B.U.H) has made the officers/administrators accountable to the people on the occasions of Haj and this practice of Hisab (Accountability) was established.

vi. Hazrat Abu Bakar (May Allah be please with him) on his election as Caliph said, "So if I act rightly, help me and if I am wrong, correct me." He further directed " Obey me when I obey Allah and his prophet Mohammad (P.B.U.H) and when I disobey Allah and his prophet Mohammad (P.B.U.H), then I have no right of obedience from you"

vii. Hazrat Umer (M.A.B.P.H) on his appointment as Caliph said, "I have entrusted in regard to your affairs. I am an individual like any one of you." He further illustrated this on some other occasion and said, "Verily my relationship with your wealth is like that of a guardian of an orphan"

viii. . Likewise hazarat Ali (M.A.B.P.H) on his appointment said " in whatever I command you, if there is obedience to Allah, it is your duty to obey me whether you like it or dislike it, and whenever I command your which involves disobedience of Allah, then there is no obedience to anyone, me or any other"

ix. The practice of accountability as

established by the prophet of Islam ((P.B.U.H) and followed by his successors is well illustrated in the annual of history. The relationship between the administrator and the citizen has been further elucidated in the sayings of the Holy Prophet (P.B.U.H) that "The nation or government can not achieve salvation, where the rights of the depressed, destitute and suppressed are not guarded and where mighty and powerful persons are not forced to accede to their rights".

x. The first Caliph Hazrat Abu Bakar (May Allah be pleased with him), in his Khutba (address) given on the assumption of office said " The weaker amongst you will be the strongest before me till I have restored to him his rights and the strongest will be weakest in my eyes till I have extracted from him what he forcibly wrested from others"

xi. Hazrat Umar (R.A) had proclaimed it throughout the Muslim World that who ever suffered oppression at the hands of any public functionary, may approach him during the Haj season. He had likewise ordered his governors to meet him on this occasion. Whenever it as proved that an officer of the state had been unjust or oppressive, he was punished promptly and the rights of the oppressed were fully restored.

xii. The importance accorded by Hazrat Ali (May Allah be pleased with him) to enforcing administrative accountability through hearing of complaints and redressal of grievances has been reflected in his famous epistle to Malik Ashter, the Governor to meet him on this occasion. Whenever it was proved that an officer of the state had been unjust or oppressive, he was punished promptly and the rights of the oppressed were fully restored.

2. Initiating of Ombudsman's Institution

i. Aristotle in his famous book "Republic" defined the justice as an act of distinction i.e. what is lawful or what is fair and equal. It is according to him, either distributive or remedial. The Two-fold ideology of the justice therefore rests on taking corrective measures to remedy the wrong and in the restoration of the rights. The absence of any regular Mohtasib (Ombudsman) or of any authority of like designation can also be attributes to the fact that every one right from the Caliph (ruler) down to an ordinary citizen was performing his duty of censor of public morals.

ii. The era of Right Caliphs, this was spread over about 27 years. Was followed by the era of Umaiyads and then by Abbasids up to 847 AD and during all these dynasties the domain of "Khilafat" was extended to the vast areas of the Middle East in Asia in th North Eastern Africa and even in Europe up to Spain.. The system was institutionalized in the era of Abbasids (750-847 AD) and DIWAN-UL-MUZALIM (Secretariat/Office of handling complaints of high handedness and oppression) was established. This Diwan-ul-Muzalim, which was headed by a capable senior judge, examined the complaints brought by the people against government officials.

iii. During the Turkish Regime, the head of the

institution was "Quadi-ul-Qadat" (The judge of judges- Chief Justice) and this alone show how much importance was attached to this institution. Even today in Saudi Arabia, this task is entrusted to the " Board of Grievances" and its members enjoys judicial privileges of such and institution with the status of a Supreme Court judge,

iv. The institution of Quad-ul-Qudat was the pioneer institution, which later on was adopted in various developed and developing countries with different names and designations. The above institution had for the first time influenced the King Charles XII of Sweden who established the

Ombudsman's institution in 1809. Dr. Pickle- the Australian Ombudsman was full of appreciation as to how the Turkish institution of Quadi-ul-Qudat adopted in Sweden came out to be the "home of Ombudsman", which later on copied with suitable amendments and modifications in various countries in Europe. The main function of the office was to ensure that laws status was followed and the civil servants fulfilled their obligations. His office was later on called "The office of the King's Chancellor of Justice".

v. Since last three or four decades, the Scandinavian office of Ombudsman has become a model for the democratic world. The institution has been accepted as an affective and important device for controlling the bureaucracy. The Ombudsman in Sweden being an Officer of Parliament investigates the complaints against the government departments on behalf of parliament for suitable remedy if on investigation the complaints against the government departments on behalf of Parliament for suitable remedy of in investigation the same are found justified. Finland has incidentally copied the Swedish ombudsman with almost all of its salient characteristics and hence both Sweden and Finland are now known as Home

Countries for helping and protecting the citizen against arbitrariness of the bureaucracy. From here the concept of accountability traveled to Denmark in 1995, followed by Norway and New Zealand in 1962. The establishment of like institution is now being favorably considered in various other European & Asian countries of the world despite their much different constitutional structure and requirement.

3. THE RAISON DE'TRE (RATIONALE)

i. There is no society without such tendencies and hence there is no government where people have no grievances against the governmental machinery. Accordingly a civilized society will have to come up with an affective mechanism for the resolution of the grievances felt by its members as well as for protecting their civic rights. Naturally such a mechanism is one where the concept of accountability is deeply ingrained. Aliksander Solzhenitsyn aptly explains this in the following words.

"Once can build the Empire state building, discipline the Russian army, make a state hierarchy mightier than God, he fail to overcome the unaccountable superiority of certain human beings"

ii. The Supreme Court of Canada in its judgment (B.C. Development Corporation V.S. Friendmann 1985 W.W.R. 193) had also considered the Ombudsman's institution " a society's inevitable requirement capable to effectively handle the problems confronting the people despite the traditional bureaucratic control devices"

CHAPTER 3

OMBUSDMAN AS CUSTODIAN OF THE RIGHTS OF THE SOCIETY

Chapter III

Chapter III

OMBUSDMAN AS CUSTODIAN OF THE RIGHTS OF THE SOCIETY

The institution of Ombudsman has emerged as a sinequa none of people's welfare.

i. The system is no longer in its developing stage and is now universally regarded as an effective device for controlling the bureaucracy. It is an important institution of the Parliament in most of the countries in the west. This has made the institution equally acceptable even to the arrogant and misbehaving bureaucracy.

ii. The Ombudsman by and large is a potent and versatile weapon. Normally the Ombudsman by and large is a potent and versatile weapon.

Normally the Ombudsman in most of the countries are concerned with his reformatory role and take steps to put the wayward bureaucracy and other governmental machinery on track and seldom overturns a decision if finds FTO be erroneous, as the overturning are mostly left to the concerned departments themselves.

iii. The labour parties in Europe and so Newzealand were initially highly critical and opposed to the Ombudsman system. They viewed that the system would ten to benefit the wealthy and rich in their rear-guard actions. “It took time to convice the labour parties who were then persuaded by the arguments of the Civil Service Unions who had feared that Ombudsman would add to their problems and feed public attitudes already inclined to be unfriendly towards the civil servant".

iv. Though the concept of Ombudsman in its present from has taken concrete shap recently late in the 20th century. Still a large section of population in the world has yet to take benefit of the system and feel protected from the indifferent and arrogant bureaucracy. The neighbouring countries in the Europe i.e. in Denmark first readily accepted the Scandinavian system in 1956, and then with a gap of six/seven years in

Norway. Newzealand in162 thereafter followed the system. In Asia, it came quite late. In Pakistan the Martial Law Administrator first appointed the Ombudsman in 1983 conspicuously. It is however a redeeming feature that establishment of Ombudsman like institution, has either been established or being actively considered in countries as far apart and as different in constitutional structure as Canada, Britain, Holland, India, Ireland, Bangladesh, Sri Lanka, Philippines, Japan, united States and several other countries. The system in most of these countries is already successfully operation and providing relief and protection to the citizen from the arbitrariness of the Government agencies. It, however, does not mean that the institution Ombudsman has received approval universally and has become by now acceptable to all the Governments. In fact the institution has not yet received the fair deal it deserves from various government in the world. Even in Pakistan though the system was established in 1983, two provinces namely NWFP Baluchistan are still hesitant to establish the offices of the Ombudsman. The Ombudsman's system requires be publicizing and discussing at various forums to dispel the misconception.

v. Ombudsman is not only a redresser of the grievances of the people at large. He is basically the guardian of law and Counselor to the Agencies when he examines and verifies the correctness of their action in a very informal manner. It should frankly be admitted that the Ombudsmen in Pakistan have so far given a good account of themselves against the stiffest odds, inadequate staff, budgetary constraints and lack of necessary legal powers to enforce implementation of their decisions.

CHAPTER 4

NATURE OF GRIEVANCES & THE MEANING, CONCEPT AND SCOPE OF "MALADMINISTRATION"

Chapter IV

Chapter IV

1. NATURE OF GRIEVANCES

It is both a matter of fact and history that in any system of government a decision making authority must create inequities. Things are however much different when the liberties of a citizen are not preserved and protected against the arbitrary and capricious authority of the state agencies. The things then tend to become too complex. All the countries of the world had increased their scope of power over their citizen. The government functions are no longer confined to the collection of revenues and maintenance of law and order. As the scale of the government functions in the administrative development and social sectors widened, the government control and growing involvement even in sectors.

2. CATEGORIS OF GRIEVANCES:

MR Geofferry Sawer, has classified the following three categories, in his treatise on "Ombudsman"

i. Such complaints which arise due to aversion and dislike of whole Collective trend or at least its particular impact on vested interest of the complainants and established beliefs.

ii. The second category grievance pertains to such actions of a department or official which in some respect are oppressive in the sense of going beyond which the lawful policy authorizes or should reasonably be interpreted as authorizing.

iii. Thirdly are the complaints those who expected to obtain a particular Item of welfare from the state and have been disappointed.

3. THE CONCEPT AND SCOPE OF "MALADMINISTRATION"

Chapter IV

i. The first commissioner (parliamentary ombudsman in great Britain) had treated the mal-administration a dirty word with unfortunate associations of such actions like taking a bribe or extreme examples of bias and perversity. The procedural mistake typographical

ii. The first commissioner (Parliamentary Ombudsman in Great Britain) had treated the mal-administration a filthy word with undesirable connection of such actions like taking a bride or great example of bias and perversity. The practical mistake hardly warranted the use of such a authoritarian term. For such small mistakes, the form commonly used in day-to-day practice is different. They are termed as “administrative lapse” or “defeat in administration” or “regularizable flaw”. In fact these are such lapses, which do not seriously and adversely affect the fundamental right of citizen or cause or impose physical or financial loss to any individual. Terminology apart, mal-administration as explained in the above, relics the key concept of all the Ombudsman‘s Act & Laws followed in the countries where such a system had already been introduced. In the short only such lapses, which are international and which had sustained injustice on an individual, are sheltered under the definition of "mal-administration" and encourage interference of the Ombudsman.

4. MAL-ADMINISTRATION OF EXECTIVE ACTION

The following actions of the executive can be regarded as mal-administration:

i. Assorted mistakes, errors and oversights

ii. Giving inaccurate information and misleading advice to the decision taking authority. This includes willful subtraction and concealment of facts and previous decisions on the subject.

iii. Failing to import information or provide inadequate explanations.

iv. Misapplication of departmental rules and instructions.

v. Pre-emptive or in-considerate behavior on the part of the officials. This includes snubbing attitude of the officers concerned and the right of patient hearing and cross examination of the relevant officer, and denial of supply of copies of relevant documents necessarily required by him to defend or present his case.

vi. The discriminatory treatment in the identical cases.

vii. Unjustifiable delay. Incidentally of all the above noted forms of mal-administration of mal-administration. Mostly the decision-making authorities in the agencies take shelter in the lack of any provision in the law or the rules or even time, which may enjoin them to dispose of a representation within a specified time. This single factor has become a potent cause of corruption amongst the bureaucracy and of frustrations amongst the general public.

3. *MAL-ADMINSTRATION AND DISCRETIONARY DECISIONS*

i. The departments as a substance of fact are vested with most of the discretionary powers of government and in the process of decision making the relevant officers take full advantage of those provisions which include no regular or planned procedure to which an applicant can press to safe an independent consideration and again reconsideration at the stage of review. The supposition is that if an official acts beyond powers or in a manner amounting to an abuse of power, then alone the aggrieved person will have a right to get redress from the Law Courts.

ii. The discretion is generally used under some critical situation by the competent authority rightly in the interest of people. The discretionary decisions are questioned and cause grievance to the general public when the decision is either taken under the impulse some corporal benefit or when right or interest of some more deserving individual is ignored or when the public interest is overlooked and made deferential to some other thought. It is rather the way the decision had been reached is challenged and not the decision itself.

It is also experiential that mostly maladministration related with the discretionary decisions are by far the result of faulty precedence or of some bad rule which create room for both exemptions and for by-passing the merit.

4 - *MAL-ADMINISTRATION WITHOUT CAUSIN INJUSTICE*

Such instances of administrative lapses are rare and are the outcome on a number of occasions due to some technical error, which in the ultimate process do not cause any injustice to the aggrieved person, though it do cause inconvenience and annoyance to him Such procedural defects are not regarded as mal-administration by the ombudsman and hence warrant simple reprimand only.

5 - *MAL-ADMINISTRATION AS DEFINED IN THE ACTS.*

i. What might and should be counted, as mal-administration is a relevant element to invoke the intervention of the Ombudsman. The ombudsman's Acts themselves provide possible help and assistance in the matter. Like other Ombudsman Laws in the world, the Ombudsman in Pakistan has also been empowered to deal with various manifestations of mal-administration.

ii. Different facets of mal-administration as included in Article 2 sub-article (2) of the

Chapter IV

Establishment of Wafaqi Mohtasib (Ombudsman) ordinance 1983) and identical provision incorporated in the provincial Acts are reproduced as under:

Article 2 Sub-article (2) of the Wafaqi Mohtasib (Ombudsman)
Ordinance 1983 (President's Ord: No.1 of 1983.

"Mal-administration"

Includes:

i. A decision, recommendations, acts of omission or commission which:

   a) Is contrary to law, rules or regulations or is a departure from established practice ore procedure, unless it is bonafide and for valid reasons or.

b) Is perverse, arbitrary or unreasonable, unjust, biased, oppressive or discriminatory or

c) Is based on irrelevant grounds or

d) Involves the exercise of powers or the failure or refusal to do so for corrupt or improper motives, such as bribery, Jobbery, favouritism, nepotism, and administrative excesses, and

ii. Neglect, inattention, delay, incompetence, inefficiency and ineptitute, in the administration or discharge of duties and responsibilities."

iii. In short, it is the particular duty of the Ombudsman to ensure that administrative authorities and others executives (only such officials who are subject to supervision of the of the Ombudsman) observe the provisions of the instrument of government concerning objectivity and impartiality and that the fundamental rights and freedom of citizens are not encroached upon in the process of public administration. Wafaqi Mohtasib – Justice(R) Shakurul Salam in his Annual Report, 1997 has identified following general aspects of mal-administration:

(a) Violation of Rules

It is a very common complaint and has been experiential in most of the cases. Either the rules/regulations in their true sense are not followed or at times used as tools to deny the relief provided for tin the rules or law under which the rules are framed. The principle that beneficial legislation is to be construed or interpreted liberally is disregarded intentionally.

(b) **Favoritism and Nepotism.**

"Favouritism" and "Nepotism" lead to twin maladies, there is violation of trust reposed in the Agency by the state, Secondly, it creates a feeling of resources less and sense of frustration in the complainant. This ultimately led to depression or aggression resulting in non-productivity and violence.

(c) **Misuse of Power**

Extraneous consideration creep into the process of decision-making power is quite often used to thwart doing the thing in a correct manner. Discretionary powers are used arbitrarily and fancifully.

(d) **Irrelevant objections**

Public is generally put to inconvenience and great trouble by means of raising irrelevant objections on their genuine demands for ulterior purposes. Mostly illiterate, or simple people coming from rural areas are the victim of such acts of mal-administration. Applicants are made to visit office frequently for trivial matters.

(e) Illegal Gratification

Mal-administration is committed mostly for the sake of illegal gratification. Because of wide spread corruption public have come to believe that nothing can be got done from public authorities except by paying bribe.

(f) Neglect of Duty

Neglect of duty and inefficiency create problems for the public. This breeds apathy to perform duty, which is pervasive.

The task of determining mal-administration is therefore quite arduous and awesome for the Ombudsman who fined it a tight rope walking against the powerful bureaucracy. Through his decisions and directives, the Ombudsman furnishes to the Agencies guidelines (some of which reproduced below) of far reaching consequences if followed earnestly and honestly. The observance of these guidelines by the agencies would surely go a long way to minimize the instances of mal-administration.

VI- GUIDELINES FOR THE AGENCIES TGO MINIMIZE MALADMINISTRATION

Following may be treated as guidelines if not fully to avoid then at least to minimize mal-administration.

1. Decisions on miscellaneous applications and complaints should be given promptly and within reasonable time.
2. All the affected parties should be heard before giving a decision.
3. The decision should be given in good faith and reflect equity and justice.
4. Reasons for the decisions should be invariably given

in clear and explicit language.

Incidentally the Ombudsman's above experience is restricted to the examining of complaints received from the public, His supervision through inspections, suo-motu actions and studies on burning subjects afflicting the life of the citizen which sometimes are not pursued vigorously for certain administrative, financial and political reasons, may further update the list of various manifestations of mal-administration.

CHAPTER 5

JURISDICTION AND POWERS

Chapter V

Chapter V

1) JURISDICTION AND POWERS REGARDING THE AIM AND OBJECTIVES OF THE SYSTEM

The institution has been established with the sole objectives that the Ombudsman popularly known as 'MOHTASIB' in Pakistan would act as a guardian of people's common and individual rights as against the arbitrariness of the government functionaries of the government and other organizations under its control. There is no change in the concept or in its objective even after about 200 years ago. However, the jurisdiction in certain countries has expanded to cover all conceivable spheres whereas in certain countries his jurisdiction has been restricted and narrowed in response to their socio political considerations. Even his duties in the society of today, has varied and discharged in a different way.

2) IN SWEDEN AND OTHER EUROPEAN COUNTRIES

Initially in the European countries, the Ombudsman was a prosecutor in proceedings judges and civil servants. In the year 1713, the King Charles XII who had been in exile in Turkey, had picked up the concept of a legal forum where people could go for the redress of their grievances. He on return decreed the appointment of a supreme representative of King Later designated as "Chancellor of Justice" with function to supervise the actions of the government officials. The "Chancellor of Justice" was however handicapped since he was not independent enough to be in a position to protect the citizen sufficiently and substantially. Accordingly in response to public opinion, the post was upgraded in 1809 and designated as "Justice Ombudsman" commonly addressed as J.O. His exhaustive powers then reflected in his functions requiring him to supervise how judges, government officials and other civil servants observe the laws with necessary powers to prosecute those who have either acted illegally or indulged in favoritism and discrimination. J.O (Swedish Ombudsman) henceforth as per Swedish Constitution, enjoyed exaulted position of the representative of the parliament and thereby of the citizen. This role of the Ombudsman was deemed a sufficient preventive measure and the purpose was achieved by the general impact of the prosecution.

i. The above procedure was subsequently replaced with the practice of reminder to the defaulting agencies with beneficial results as the agencies adopted right course to mitigate the sufferings and resolve the grievances in the light of his elaborately argued reminders. In Pakistan and other Asian countries, the defaulting agencies are either issued "directive" or recommendations having the force of a decision, if on investigation adequate prima facie case has been made out and mal-administration substantiated.

3) SUPERVISORY ROLE

i. The extent of success of the ombudsman is therefore largely depended upon his extent of jurisdiction and power. The Swedish Act of parliamentary Ombudsman enacted on 13th November 1986, has spelled out his supervisory role and jurisdiction in section 2as under:

i. Jurisdiction over state and local government authorities; and

ii. Officials and other employees of the above mentioned authorities;

iii. Also oversees other persons holding posts and assignments entailing the exercise of public authority; and

iv. Officials and holders of assignments in state business

and administrative authorities (e.g. the State telecommunications, general administration) when on their employers behalf, exercise powers in matters where the state has a decisive influence."

ii. The jurisdiction of the Swedish ombudsman has also been extended to the Armed Forces. However the supervision shall apply only to officers in the ranks not lower than that of the second lieutenant and those holding equivalent positions.

iii. It is an essential function of the Swedish Ombudsman to ensure that courts of law and administrative authorities observe the provisions of the instrument of government concerning objectivity and impartiality and that the fundamental rights and freedom of citizens are not encroached upon in the processes of public administration. Ombudsman shall also pay attention to the forms and manner in which local government autonomy is conducted.

4) GUARDIAN OF LAW

i. The peculiar aspect of the jurisdiction which the Swedish Ombudsmen exercise relates to their taken action (Section 4 of the Swedish Act of Instructions 1986) to remedy deficiencies in legislation, if while performing supervision duties, the amendment in any legislation or any other measure is considered essential for the dispensation of justice based on equity and good governance. For this, the Ombudsman may make a reference on the subject to the government or Riksdag (parliament).

ii. The examination and investigations into the

complaints received from the public constitute normal duties of the Ombudsman are vast enough to merit him the title of the "guardian of law". If by means of a complaint against an official or of by other means such as through the press, the Ombudsman (JK) becomes aware of aware of an act of mismanagement or mal-administration, he is bound to have an inquiry made and if justified by the investigation, to have the official prosecuted in the court.

5- *SUO-MOTO POWERS EXERCISE BY THE OMBUDSMAN IN PAKISTAN*

i. The ombudsman in Pakistan thought not beard by the law to investigate suo-moto any act of mal-administration coming to this notice by the media or by any other reliable source, does not find himself duty bound to take cognizance of the same and accordingly may opt to ignore several of such reporting in the press or received from any source for personal or for socio-political grounds without assigning any reason for the same. In other words, in normal course, it is not obligatory for the ombudsman in Pakistan to compulsorily institute inquiry of his own respect of administrative lapses, bureaucratic bungling, and disregard of the law and rules even if reported in the press. Similarly it is not incumbent upon the ombudsman to ensure prosecution of the delinquent official even if the guilt is proved after investigation. However nothing deters him from making a special report to the appropriate quarters in government for initiating suitable action under the efficiency and discipline rules or under any other appropriate law. Again action or no action on the Ombudsman's report is the absolute discretion of the government. However like other ombudsmen or parliamentary Commissioners, the Ombudsman in Pakistan, if the magnitude of the guilt or omission is of less significance, may take a lenient view and let the matter stand as it is after nothing serious has been see in the explanation of the agency and after a correction or remedial action has been bought about by the respondent agency.

6- INSPECTION OF THE AGENCIES

Apart from the fact that the Swedish J.O (Ombudsman) very often initiates investigation without being motivated by a complaint, he frequently checks the work of the officials while he is on inspection tours. The inspection of the agencies under his jurisdiction is an important sphere of his activity. Every year he or his assistant visits courts, prosecutors, police authorities, and government officials of all types. The inspection includes interviews of the officers, discussion and examination of random documents and thus, the J.O satisfies himself with regard to prompt and proper disposal of the complaints of the people. Mere hello and chitchat with the visitors found in the offices of the government, gives him sufficient insight about the problems of the people, the delays in the implementation of the decisions and the inconveniences and the objectionable demean our of the officials. The J.O also personally inspects jails, guardrooms, mental hospitals, wine shops, and other institutions of alcoholics, and homes for way ward children. Through conversations with the officials, and inmates of the above institutions he meets on each visit, the Ombudsman (J.O) ascertains for himself whether or not inmates are being properly treated.

Incidentally all the Federal and Provincial Acts of Ombudsman in Pakistan have more or less identical provisions but for unexplained reasons, they are not religiously acted upon. The Ombudsman normally finds himself under obligation to investigate into such subjects and matters of alleged mall-administration; only which are referred to him by the President/Governor or by the Supreme or High Courts or even by the Parliament or Provincial Assemblies. In such cases, which are referred to him, he does not initiate any remedial action in pursuance of his own findings and instead remains contended after he has sent his findings to the referring authority for his suitable action. The ombudsman's Laws in Pakistan as envisaged in Articles 17 & 18 provide constitution of Inspection

Teams and Standing Committees etc. But for reasons not defined in the annual reports, no effective measure has so far been taken to meet the purpose of these provisions. Perhaps public involvement, for fear of politicization is shun and not yet considered appropriate in the interest of the institution. However Provincial ombudsman Sindh Justice R Hazif-ul –Khairi has constituted two officials member inspection teams for the inspection of institution run under the control of the Health and Education Departments of Govt. of Sindh.

7- POWER OF PROSECUTION

The Swedish Ombudsman is also invested with the powers of prosecution, whenever a case of arrogance or improper conduct is reported to him. This is not compliance of his directions during the course of investigation whereas in the case of Swedish Ombudsman these powers relate to the immensely behavior and rude treatment shown to the public by the non-responsive official. In fact it is the disregard of the legal rights and criminal in –attention of the agencies, which are liable to prosecution by the Ombudsman and if the individual complaint has sustained damages as well due to the error of the officials of the agency, then on establishment of guilt, the complainant has all the opportunities to claim damages. Serious view; is taken, if the same concerns high officers who despite better intelligence. Education and experience fail to act properly and lawfully. This provides greater legal security to the people at large, In Pakistan, there is a comparable provisions in Article 22 of the Ombudsman, s Law which empowers the Ombudsman, if deems necessary, to call upon a public servant, other functionary or any agency to show cause why compensation be not awarded to an aggrieved party for any loss or damage suffered by them on account of any mal-administration committed by such public servant, other functionary or agency. In the event of no satisfactory explanation, Ombudsman may award reasonable costs or compensation and the same shall be recoverable as arrears of land revenue from; the delinquent public servant, functionary or agency. The Ombudsman also follows up to see if the injured parities have been compensated. The Swedish Ombudsman is however quite mindful about such cases and so always instructs the prosecutor, to give the wronged person; free legal aid in claiming damages. No prosecution is however ordered by him for excusable faults and instead gives the erring official an opportunity to give redress to the aggrieved person. When no personal liability of an official is established, the Swedish Ombudsman may also appeal to the government for compensation to he complainant and such a request is invariably acceded to by the government. Such are the cases when an innocent citizen is hit in a shoot out exercise carried out against the bandits and a follow up investigation could not determine the police officer at fault.

8- INTERVENTION TO ENSURE FREEDOM OF MOVEMENT

The Ombudsman invokes his powers even in matters when the legislator, without very str4ong reasons, gives the administrator powers to introduce general instructions on the citizen's movements liable to lead to prohibition for which there was no real cause. These powers are however, exercised by him very sparingly.

9- POWERS AND JURISDICTION AS ENSHRINED IN OMBUDSMAN ACTS/ORDERS IN PAKISTAN.

As already stated earlier, the Provinces have scrupulously followed the provisions of the Federal Ombudsman's (Mohtasib) Order (President Order No.1 of 1983). The little variation and modifications found in the Acts of the Province of Punjab and Azad Jammu & Kashmir are not material.

Chapter V

The reproduction of the relevant Articles of the Federal Mohtasib (Ombudsman Presidential order NO. .1 of 1983 adopted by the provincial Acts in Verbatim, will perhaps be appropriate to further grasp the dimensions of the jurisdiction and powers of the Ombudsmen in Pakistan in comparison to the Ombudsmen and other like institutions in other countries of the world.

The scanning of the decisions and other material incorporated in the annual reports ;of the Federal Mohtasib show that powers to proceed under contempt Act or powers as incorporated in Article 13, 15, and 23 (1) & (2) are either not or seldom invoked by the Ombudsman, thereby establishing that, by and large the agencies had responded positively and co-operated with the investigation officers. The annual reports of the Federal Mohtasib (Ombudsmen) however do not provide the statistical information with regard to the references, which Mohtasib (Ombudsmen) had made to various agencies and how for those references were investigated and complied with by the concerned agencies. Likewise no information of penal actions or of contempt proceedings instituted by him appears in the Annual Reports of the Ombudsman.

Incidentally; the author has the privilege of remaining associated with the Provincial Ombudsmen (Mohtasib) Sindh since its inception and had also worked as Acting Ombudsman during the intervening period of the first two regular Ombudsmen during the intervening period of the first two regular Ombudsmen. During the tenure of the First Ombudsmen, studies mainly on the working of Karachi Building Control Authority and Financial Mismanagement of the Local Councils in Sindh; were conducted and during the tenure of the Second Ombudsmen a good number of investigations were held and recommendations submitted on the references received; from the Governor of Sindh. The details of those studies carried out during 1991 – 1995 and the references of the Governor of Sindh dealt during 1995-1998 are incorporated in the annual reports of the respective years. It is astonishing that the Ombudsmen's Secretariat received no information from the government about the action taken on those reports and hence finds no mention of the same in the same in the respective annual reports. Incidentally the annual reports of the Provincial Ombudsmen Punjab and Jammu & Azad Kashmir are also deficient in respect of the above information.

10- MATTERS WHERE JURISDICTION IS OUSTED

i) The position as existed in Sweden has been specifically discussed in detail since Sweden has been regarded as 'Home Country of Ombudsmen'. The topic would remain incomplete, if the agencies and the matters where the jurisdiction of the Swedish Ombudsmen has been ousted is not examined and critically compared with Pakistan simultaneously.

ii) The Swedish Ombudsmen do not exercise supervision over the members of the Riksdag (Pakistan). There is no such ouster clause in the Ombudsmen Laws in Pakistan. In Pakistan Mohtasib can look into the alleged acts of mal-administration of the minister, advisers and Parliamentary Secretaries in addition to other public servants. The public servants as defined in Article 2 Sub Article 6 of the Wafaqi Mohtasib (Ombudsmen) Ordinance 1983 and Section 2 Sub Section 2 Sub Section 6 of the Sindh Ombudsmen's Act, 1991, includes a Minister, Advisor, Parliamentary Secretary in addition to the Chief executives of any organization, Director, Officers, and other employees of an agency. However the above Acts are silent in respect of the prime Minister, Chief Ministers, Chairman Senate or Speakers of the national and Provincial Assemblies.

iii) The Swedish ombudsman has jurisdiction over the Administrative Board of Riskdag, The Riskdag Election Court, and Riskdag Appeal Boards. Likewise the Ombudsman Laws in Pakistan have not created any jurisdiction of the Ombudsmen over the senate, National and Provincial Assemblies or the Committees constituted by these organizations on various subjects.

a. The Ombudsman does not supervise each other. Due regard is given reciprocally in Pakistan as well.

b. The Governing Board of the Bank of Sweden, the Governor and the Deputy Governors of the Bank do not fall within the purview of the Swedish Ombudsman of the matter does concern participation in the exercise of the Bank's right of decision in accordance with the Foreign Exchange Act (SFS-1990-749) and the Act on payment to and from Foreign Countries (SFS-1990-

750). There is no such specific immunity granted in the relevant Ombudsman's Act in Pakistan.

c. The jurisdiction of the Swedish Ombudsman is ousted against Cabinet Ministers.

d. The justice chancellor is also not within the purview of the Ombudsman. No Ombudsman in Pakistan shall have any jurisdiction to investigate or inquire into any matter, which are subjdice before a court of competent jurisdiction or judicial tribunal or Board on the date of receipt of complaint.(Article 9 of the President's Order No .1 and Section 9 Sub section a proviso, 1983)

11- BAR OF JURISDICTION

I) On the other hand as provided under Article 29 of the Federal Ombudsman Order 1983 and Section 29 of the Provincial Ombudsman in

Sindh Act, 1991 no court or other authority shall have jurisdiction.

i- to question the authority of action taken, or intended to be taken or order made, or any thing done or purporting to have been taken, made or done under this act or

ii- to grant an injunction or stay or to make any interim order in relation to any proceedings before or any thing done or intended to be done or purporting have been done by, or under the orders or at instance of the Ombudsman.

II) There is no comparable Article of section 8 of the Swedish Act of Instruction to the Parliamentary

Ombudsman (1986) in Pakistan. It provides that the Ombudsmen should not take action against subordinate officials who are not vested with independent powers, unless this is called far on special grounds. Though no such specific provision exists in the Ombudsman's Acts in Pakistan, yet in practice no non-gazetted officer/subordinate officer is put to task for any ordinary lapse. However no head of office or any high-ranking officer who in several matters is a decision-making authority is responsible for any order is passed on the files is in the ordinary course seldom held responsible or prosecuted for the mal-administration and mal–practices. The practice of the finding the lower functionaries responsible for the proven mal-administration to save the superior needs to be discouraged. Indecently no instance of disciplinary action or prosecution instituted against any senior officer of the level of Secretary to Government or any Chief of the autonomous body or corporation is cited in the Annual Reports of the Ombudsman in Pakistan. Contempt notices were of course issued which latter on were vacated either on their furnishing the explanation or on providing the due redress to the complaint. In fact decision-making authorities in Pakistan take shelter behind the office noticing of the officers down below who are very often made scapegoat on such occasions. It has also been observed that in certain cases notings leading to an incorrect, malafide orders are tailored at the instance and verbal instruction of the decision making authorities. Accordingly providing law to protect the sub-ordinate officials as found in Swedish Law appears to be appropriate to ward off such a mal-practice.

III) All courts, judicial tribunals or Boards lie outside the jurisdiction of the Ombudsmen in Pakistan. The Swedish Ombudsmen are on the contrary empowered to prosecute a member of the Supreme Court or the Supreme Administrative Court in pursuant to the instructions of Parliament. He may even institute proceedings concerning the removal or debarment of such a member from his post.

12- OTHER SPECIFIC AREAS WHERE JURISDICTION IS OUSTED.

The jurisdiction of the Ombudsmen in Pakistan has also been ousted in to any matter which:

i) Relate to the external affairs of Pakistan or the relations or dealing of Pakistan with any foreign state or Government (Article 9(b). He is however not debarred from investigating into the complaints filed by foreign national against the Agencies under his jurisdiction. The Ombudsman in other countries as well does not exercise the jurisdiction in matters relating to the external affairs of their country.

ii) Relate to, or connected with the defence of Pakistan or any part thereof, the military, naval and air forces of Pakistan or the matters covered by the laws relating to those forces (Article 9(c).

iii) The law was not clear the jurisdiction of the Ombudsmen in respect of such institutions/organizations which were governed/controlled by the Ministry of Defence but in practice were engaged in the work of civil nature like the Defence but in practice were engaged in the work of civil nature like the Defence Housing Authorities, M.F.R .O, and other foundations of the forces. The Chief Martial Law Administrator's Secretariat Pakistan vide its order dated 13th August, 1984 had widened the scope of the ouster as contained in paragraph of proviso to clause (I) of Article 9 of the Establishment of the office of Wafaqi Mohtasib (Ombudsmen) Order. 1983. The ouster of jurisdiction is now absolute in respect of the following.

> "The Defence division, the defense Production Division and the Military, naval, or air forces of Pakistan and any department, body, authority or organization directly or indirectly under the management or control of or in any manner connected with either of the said Division or the said forces".

The ouster had left no option to a civilian to seek remedy from the ombudsman in the event he has been seriously erred by any official of the above organizations because of its non-transparent and misconceived actions. Civilian members of the Defense of its non-transparent and misconceived seek redress for the alleged wrongs done to them by these bodies or by the Builders and Developers whose activities are controlled and over seen by such authorities.

13- JURISDICTION OF THE OMBUDSMAN IN 'SERVICE MATTER'

The ouster of the jurisdiction of the Ombudsmen about the complaints by or on behalf of public servant or functionary concerning any personal matters relating to the agency in which he or she is or has been working is however controversial. The Ombudsmen under Article 9 sub Art(2) has been restrained to accept any complaint where the grievance of a civil servant relates to his service, as ordinarily for such grievances a judicial forum named as " Civil Services Tribunal", has already been provided at the Federal and Provincial levels.

Chapter V

14- AREAS EXCLUDED FROM THE JURISDICTION

The plain reading of Article 1(2) of the President's Order No.1 of 1983 envisage that the jurisdiction of the Wafaqi Mohtasib (Ombudsmen) was initially extended to the whole of Pakistan without exception so that no citizen of any area is deprived of the facility of cheap and prompt redressal of the grievance. That after one year of the promulgation of the Wafaqi Mohtasib Order 1983, for special reasons of tribal traditions and customs, the President vide Notification dated 13th August, 1984 had excluded all maters relating to, or connected directly or indirectly with the Federally administrated Tribal Areas from the operation and purview of all provisions of the Wafaqi Mohtasib (Ombudsmen) Order 1983. The ouster of jurisdiction was not restricted to the institution of Ombudsmen only, but even the Article 247(7) of the constitution of Islamic Republic of Pakistan, bans the Supreme Court and the High Court from exercising any Since no law to the contrary has been enacted so far in this behalf, the High Courts inclusive of the Ombudsmen in Pakistan have no jurisdiction as far as tribal areas are concerned.

15- FINDINGS AND RECOMMENDATIONS

The discussion on jurisdiction and power would be incomplete if the controversial view existing on the above subject is also not simultaneously deliberated. Admittedly the very presence of mal-administration is the sole criteria and basis for the Ombudsman to order investigations/inquiry into admitted position that the powers of the Ombudsmen with regard to the status of findings and recommendations have generally remained the same since from the date this institution was first established in Sweden. The Ombudsmen, who is of course not a judge in the strict sense, does not have the authority to change the decision of the courts and so of the administrative officials. He will of course through his findings and recommendations provide a basis and ground for the annulment or modification of the decision in review to the officers concerned. So consciously no Ombudsmen would usurp or assume the jurisdiction of the "Appellate Authority" in disregard to the mechanism provided in the Administrative hierarchy itself. The objective is achieved if on account of the intervention of the Ombudsmen, The errant decision is modified or cause of grievance is removed. In fact, the Ombudsmen's interceding is required to compel the delinquent agency to abide by the law and refrain from acting in violation of rule and laws as well as when the action is in conflict with the norms of good governance. Further to promote the good governance and boost effectiveness of the Ombudsmen, all officials and authorities are obliged to provide him with the information they have on a matter in question. Similarly, the Ombudsmen has the right to ask for the assistance of any official in the discharge of his functions, right from the stage of investigation to the implementation of his recommendations.

The implication of this provision is all-comprehensive.

16- POWERS OF THE TEMPORARY INJUNCTION

It is very often and genuinely complained that Ombudsman is handicapped in the absence of clear power with regard to the pre-regard to the pre-rogative orders, declarations, stay orders and injunctions by which an aggrieved person could obtain an interim relief pending final adjudication of the alleged acts of mal-administration's Law. Vests in him the same powers as 14(1) of the Federal Ombudsman's Law. Vests in him the same powers as ate vested in a Civil Court under the code of civil procedure, 1908(Act V of 1908) in respect of the following matters namely;

a) Summing and enforcing the attendance of any person and examining him on oath;

b) Compelling the production of documents;

c) Receiving evidence or affidavits; and

d) Issuing commission for the examination of witnesses.

17- POWERS TO PUNISH FOR CONTEMPT

The relevant Article 16 of the Ombudsman's law which is quite comprehensive and self explanatory, invests in the Ombudsman such powers, mutatis mutandis as the Supreme Court/High Courts have to punish any person for its contempt. Such a person is one who:

a) Abuse, interferes with, impedes, imperils, or obstructs the process of the Ombudsman in any way or disobeys any order of the Ombuds man.

b) Scandali zes the Ombuds man or otherwis e or otherwis e does any thing which tends to bring the Ombuds man, himself or his nominee s or any person authoriz ed by the Ombuds man in relation to his office, into hatred, ridicule or contemp t.

c) Does anything which tends to prejudic e the determin ation of a matter pending before the Ombuds man, or

d) Does any other thing, which, by any other law, constitut es contemp t of court.

"Provided that fair comments, made in good faith and in public interest on the working of the Ombudsman or any of his staff, or on the final report of the Ombudsman after completion of the investigation's shall not constitute contempt of the Ombudsman or his office"

The above provision has insulated the Ombudsman and his staff from the derogatory activities of any person-complainant as well as agency in the discharge of its statutory functions. He has been provided with the privileges and protection, as has been conceived essential for the judges of the courts. Besides retrieving the honour and dignity of the institution, the investiture of such powers was imperative to prevent and stifle any damage to public confidence in this important organ of the state. These powers have ensured peaceful and disciplined proceedings during the investigation as well as compel the agency to comply all such orders and produce all such record which the Ombudsman or his nominated member of the staff considers necessary for the completion of the investigation.

By invoking the above provisions, the Chief Secretary or the Head of the Organization could have been asked to ensure compliance of the decision by the errant agency failing which the authority whose assistance has been sought, could have been competently proceeded against under the efficiency and discipline rules.

The above interpretation is not contributed some who argue that the above provisions are specifically provided to vest the Mohtasib (Ombudsman) with the necessary powers to complete his investigations expeditiously as well as to formulate his recommendations. It is argued that constitutional petitions without availing the remedy provided in the Ombudsman's law itself i.e. filing representation before the President invoking provision under Article 32 of P.O NO.1 of 1983 within 30 days of the decision of order. There is a clear bar of jurisdiction of courts under Article 29 to question among others as to the validity of any action taken by the learned Wafaqi Mohtasib. The legal position indicating the circumstances when Superior Courts can legitimately intervene is already discussed in the above in the above in the case of International Cargo Handling Company (Pvt) Ltd. Incidentally this decision was made in a suit but in similar situation the principles spelt out wherein will apply with greater force in constitutional jurisdiction of the High Court. The Honourable Sindh High Court in a case (P.I.A Corporation v/s

Wafaqi Mohtasib PLD 1994. Karachi -32) had refused the petitioner permission to agitate various grounds as the petitioner had not availed the remedy under Article 32 of the Wafaqi Mohtasib was able to show that the order of the Wafaqi Mohtasib was without jurisdiction.

18- Recommendations of Ombudsman are binding on the Agencies.

i) The very purpose of the creation of the office of Ombudsman lies in the implementation ;of his findings/recommendations-President and the Prime Minister of Pakistan have emphatically directed the agencies to implement the findings/recommendations of the Ombudsman and desist; from making necessary representations to the president and desist from making necessary representations to the President (Governor in the case of Provinces). Resort to representation under Article 32 of the Order instead of expeditious implementation of the recommendations of Ombudsman and thereby thwarting the ends of justice, and the Supreme Court has deprecated aggravating the sufferings of the complainants. Further the contention that the Mohtasib were recommendatory in nature and not binding on the government is in clear conflict with the directives of the President and the Prime Ministers of Pakistan.

Chapter V

CHAPTER 6

SUO-MOTU ACTION

Chapter VI

i) Besides, it has been the departmental interpretation of; the Federal Government itself that recommendations of the Mohtasib ought to be implemented promptly. The office of the Ombudsman has been created for redress of grievances of the citizen who are not in a position to approach the Courts/ Officials and the Minister concerned. Not withstanding various directives issued by the president and the Prime minister from time to time urging the Federal agencies (it includes Provincial agencies as well) to implement the order of Mohtasib (Ombudsman), a large number of representations are invariably filed and the same remain pending at that juncture. A general perception is that dilatory tactics are resorted to by the agencies/ government functionaries to see to it that the orders passed favoring the citizens are made the subject-matter of the representations under Article 32 of the order and thereby thwarting the further process/implementation thereof Supreme Court expressed its deep concern about the alarming situation with a view to alleviating the miseries of the citizens who run from pillar to post of obtain relief in terms of the orders of the Mohtasib.

ii) The exercise of these powers its still inadequate since it has been observed that the Ombudsman in Pakistan does not liverally use the provision of suo motu action. Probably because there is normally some influential hand behind most of such acts of malfeasance and misfeasance and Ombudsman avoid involving themselves in political controversies. As a result, these acts of maladministration perpetuate and constantly haunt the general public. These scars on good governance can be scrapped only when the provision of suo motu action is widely and liberally used. Various such case, which have appeared in the national dailies from time to time, may be quoted which had escaped the notice and could have invited an action by the Ombudsman.

iii) The most common acts of maladministration which have been causing concern to the society and frequently appearing in the media are listed here-under to suggest that Ombudsman in Pakistan may not await some complaint in writing from any citizen.

- Unauthorized construction and other building works.
- Unauthorized conversion of amenity plots into residential or commercial.
- Industrial or commercial activities in a purely residential area.
- Establishment of a hazardous industry or work-shop causing environmental pollution in or in

the vicinity of some residential area.

- Acts promoting pollution and endangering public health.
- Prolonged spell of water shortage and complaint of contamination or of other impurities in the drinking water.
- Collapsing sewerage system, chocked sewerage lines inundating roads and streets in the cities of Pakistan.
- Misuse of floodwater drains for the disposal of sewerage and waste in Karachi.
- Police atrocities and extortion.
- Unhygienic condition of prisons and inhuman treatment met to the prisoners.
- Mismanagement and complaints of basic services in the recently developed areas or new colonies

- Discriminatory and unethical actives in the private and public educational institutions.

iv) Only common facets of maladministration are identified in the above. In order to detect afore mentioned acts of maladministration and for their corrective measures, Ombudsman may enlist the assistance of non-government Agencies (NGO's). In fact suo motu action is aimed; too shakeup the administration and to persuade it to give up its negligent and indifferent posture towards its statutory functions. The provision of "own volition investigation" cab be used liberally to nib the nuisance in the bud or to investigate into the sources of problems or secondly to recommend preventive and remedial measures. With the exception of those measures, which cannot be implemented immediately on the ground of resource4 constraints, Agencies in the ordinary course willingly accept and implement the decisions of the Ombudsman. Much can be learnt; from the Commissioner for Administrative Complaints (COMAC) Hong Kong who liberally invoked, the suo motu provision for the overall improvement of the administration to the benefit of the citizen.

v) The trust in; this field is; seen in the case of Ombudsman Sindh who has taken bold initiative and probed into several high profile cases of corruption on his own volition. This has alerted the bureaucracy at large. His performance with a difference has earned him appreciation both from the media and public. The enquiry into the scam of allotments in New Zubzi Mandi and Malir Development Authority had unveiled startling instances of graft and corruption. Even in the social sector the suo moto cognizance of mal-administration has yielded dividend to the great relief of general public.

The campaign launched on his instructions for the elimination of pye dogs and for taking remedial measures for the treatment of dog bite cases has saved several human lives and brought relief in; the poor congested urban areas of Karachi.

vi) Needless to emphasize that the next new Millennium will be regarded more than ever for an ongoing process of a fair and clean administration. The transparency in the conduct and working of the government Agencies will be more closely watched by the citizen, hence the institution of Ombudsman will be required to gear up for the up-coming changes. He will be required to play a vital role since he is placed in a privileged position from where he is able to monitor the complaints and problem of the people, which they encounter at the hands of irresponsible and irresponsive bureaucracy. Equally, it is also important that the remedial measures recommended by the ombudsman are practicable, substantial, and concrete to meet the challenges of the ensuing millennium.

CHAPTER 7

INSPECTION AND TOURING

Chapter VII

Chapter VII

INSPECTION AND TOURING

Constitution of Inspection Teams and Advisory Committees

The inspection of the offices of the ministries and departments within the jurisdiction constitutes an important function of the Ombudsman. In fact inspection is an effective device for controlling bureaucracy.

1- CONSTITUTION OF INSPECTION TEAMS

In Pakistan article 17 of the Presidential Orders No.1 of 1983 (Wafaqi Mohtasib's (Ombudsman's) Order 1983) provides as under:-

2- INSPECTION TEAM (ARTICLE 17 OF THE PRESIDNETIAL ORDER NO.1 OF 1983)

i. The Mohtasib may constitute an Inspection Team for the performance of any of the functions of the Mohtasib.

ii. An Inspection Team shall consist of one or more members of the staff and shall be assisted by such other person or persons, as the Mohtasib May consider necessary.

iii. An inspection Team shall exercise such of the powers of the Mohtasib as he may specify by order in writing and every report of the Inspection Team shall first be submitted to the Mohtasib with its recommendations for appropriate action.

Besides the Inspection Team which he may constitute for the purpose, he can also draw programmed of his personal inspections to attach due importance to this statutory function. Incidentally he carries out no regular inspections of the agencies under his jurisdiction and perhaps no team as conceived in the act is notified so far. Reasons for ignoring this important provision are not understood though in other countries, the Ombudsman with desirable impact regularly carries out inspections. The inspections had not only brought down the number of individual complaints, but had also educated the Ombudsman in respect of such acts of maladministration which had not come to his knowledge otherwise and had needed remedial measures. The Ombudsman in Sindh in recent months had constituted a team headed by his investigating officer (a retired Medical Superintendent) to visit various hospitals and government health centers to see by himself as to how the affairs in those institutions are conducted to ameliorate the sufferings of the sick with no resources. The team had unearthed various inadequate professional conduct and detected the expired and spurious medicines and injections in the government stores.

3- INSPECTION OF THE OMBUDSMAN IN OTHER COUNTRIES

i) In Sweden the Ombudsman (J.O) inspects every public agency at least once during his tenure. Undoubtedly the complaints from the individuals when t6hey are treated unjustly by a public officer or officials, dominate the activities of the Ombudsman in Sweden, yet the inspections and his finding/ recommendations are termed as important tools to improve; the working of any office. Interestingly the government officers in Sweden take full advantage of his visits and inspections. They approach the Ombudsman (J.O) whenever they desire to have their some action examined and verified as to its correctness and the Ombudsman willingly extends the required counseling.

ii) The above position is true in other countries of the world as well.

Unlike their counter part, other countries like the Norwegian Ombudsman do not routinely inspect the institution and officer where actions may give rise to problems deserving his attention. The relevant statute of Norwegian Ombudsman provides that "he shall have access to service establishment. Offices, and other premises of all administrative organs and all enterprises which come within the province of his office". This may be taken to mean that when he is investigating, the circumstances if so warranted in any particular case, he may visit the authority concerned. This is true in the case of Pakistan Ombudsman as well.

4- WHETHER DID THE OMBUDSMAN'S SECRETARIAT IS A COMPLAINT BUREAU?

The Ombudsman's institution is more than a Complaint Bureau to which an outraged citizen may turn. He can and does proceed on his own motion. He supervises the observance of laws and statutes as the government officials may apply them. This function can be best performed when the Ombudsman periodically inspects the working of various offices of public dealing. Some jurists regard his periodic inspections as the surest guarantee for the possible transparent governance.

5- CITIZEN'S DAY AND CITIZEN HOUR

i) Accessibility to the complainants is an important attribute rather the hallmark of this institution. To achieve this, the Ombudsman has earmarked the days and citizen's hour for direct interaction with the complainants who for various personal reasons want to inform him with his woes and sufferings in person. His polite and patient hearing to those coming from the remote areas take away from them the fear and hesitation. In fact his frank discussion and heart to heart talk with the poor complainants bring solace and satisfaction to them even before their grievances are actually redressed. This provides the much-harassed complainants protection from the torture and such coercive measure of the Agencies not ordinarily conceived in the law and rules. Moreover, the complainants also the opportunity to explain the ombudsman, in case where, the investigation needs to be reappear or where, the implementation of his recommendations had been ignored or unreasonably delayed by the Agency. This also helps the Ombudsman in the upholding of the required discipline in his own secretariat too.

ii) On the citizen's "Day" and "Hour" almost all the investigating officers remain available to attend to any query of the Ombudsman and also to provide personalized briefing to the worried complaints'

iii) The practice of 'Citizen's Day' and 'Citizen's Hour' has proved a good experience since this besides establishing a healthy interaction with the people has also gone a long way to build up their confidence and faith in the institution and regard the Ombudsman as "REDRESSER" and "PROTECTOR".

6- CONSTITUTION OF ADVISORY & STANDING COMMITTEES

i) Article 18 of President's Order No.1 of 1983 empowers the Ombudsman to establish whenever he thinks fit, standing Advisory Committees at specified places with specified jurisdiction for performing such functions of the Mohtasib as may be assigned to them from time to time. No details of the constitution of such Committees are available in the Annual Reports of the Wafaqi

Mohtasib except that in 1993, Mohtasib had setup an Advisory Committee for Peshawar Region including Mardan and the Malakhand divisions. The committee comprised of well-known personalities of the Region. The committee held deliberations with various Agencies, examined cases of maladministration and suggested remedial measures and certain amendments in rules and procedure.

ii) The Ombudsman (Mohtasib) had also appointed an Advisory Committee for Karachi Zone in the same year, which had held meeting with K.E.S.C. management for suitable recommendations.

iii) In subsequent year's Annual Reports, no information about the fresh constitution of such advisory committees is found mentioned.

iv) Incidentally no such Committees are reportedly constituted in the

Provinces of Punjab and Sindh, since the Annual Reports of these institutions are silent about the same.

CHAPTER 8

COMPLAINT HANDLING

Chapter VIII

Chapter VIII

COMPLAINT HANDLING

(1) PROFESSIONAL HANDLING OF THE COMPLAINT.

i) The term Complaint Handling implies processing of complaints and if prima facie alleged allegations on initial examination lead to the commission of some sort of mal-administration by the government functionary, admits the same for regular investigation and final recommendation. Complaint handling necessary requires careful, intelligent and scientific treatment by an officer with deep insight into the law, rule, and practice, and practice. He is also supposed to be conversant with the bureaucratic ways of dealing the affairs.

ii) This chapter basically deals about the skill regarding complaint handling.

a) Complaints should be welcomed in order to prevent their occurrence. The emphasis should be on resolving the irritants and preventing their repetition.

b) All efforts should be made to gain public confidence. Even the patient listening to the complaint and adoption of measures to quickly registers the complaint for in depth investigation of the frustration of the complainant.

c) An efficient complaint cell can get most of the grievances resolved at its own level simply by making an inquisitive enquiry from the agency or by tendering an advice to the agency complained against. This in several cases provide an opportunity to the agency in taking a remedial measure as well as in perfecting the administration system of its organization. In short; a good complaint handing system will ensure that most of the complaints of ordinary nature;

not involving any complex question of law and practice, are resolved "swiftly and reliably as close to the roots of the problem as possible".

d) Complaint Cell should be easily accessible and located conspicuously in the Ombudsman's Secretariat and in its Regional Offices.

e) Due measures may be taken to publicize widely through media and office notice boards, the procedure and other requisites (Photo copies of the related documents) of the complaint. All this should be simple to invoke and operate with clearly defined stages and responsibilities. Preferably the basic instructions for filing the complaint should invariably be printed on the acknowledgement letter of the complaints/petitions both in Urdu and Regional languages. This letter should also indicate further documents needed or the action to be taken imperatively required to process the complaint for final admittance.

f) The complaint cell (Registry Department) of the Ombudsman Secretariat should be objective and free from undue influence or interference.

g) The complaint (in rare cases so as to protect the complainant's privacy) may be treated as confidential if so requested by the complainant.

h) Where some ambiguity or doubt is created with regard to jurisdiction etc, the registry section may consult the concerned investigating officer or any other senior colleague before final orders of the Ombudsman for its admittance or otherwise are obtained.

iii) Again it is quite essential that the complaint or Registry Section (whatever name is assigned by the respective organization) should have a clear concept of the complaint to determine as to what it wishes to get out of the complaint. In fact a complaint is an expression of dissatisfaction with the government organization or Department's policies, procedures, charges, employees, agents, quality of service, delays in the payment of outstanding legal dues etc.

a) Request for an appointment (employment) has been made.

b) Request is made for providing information or explanation on the policy and practice of such organization, which fall within or outside the purview of the Ombudsman.

c) Matters for which a remedy is already provided in the relevant act or where an independent appeal channel has already been provided

d) It is also important to know as to who can complain. In fact the person who is manifestly aggrieved can lodge the complaint. The complainant or where appropriately by a person duly authorized by him can lodge it personally.

e) In the ordinary course no anonymous or pseudonymous complaint is admitted for investigation. Yet it may always be useful to develop a policy to deal with anonymous complaints. An anonymous complaint can be acted on where the matter is relatively serious and there is sufficient credible information in the complaint-meriting probe.

f) A policy is always needed to deal appropriately the repetitive complaints. Such a situation may arise in respect of basic utility service like water supply sewerage, general sanitation, electricity, telephone and gas.

2- FORMS OF COMPLAINTS

i. Complaint should be made in writing on solemn affirmation or oath setting out the actual grievance and the remedy sought for.

ii. The language should be simple. Provocative or contemptuous language should be avoided.

iii. Assistance may be provided to those who have difficulty in writing down (drafting) their complaints.

iv. In most of the countries a telephone hot line has been stet up and necessary arrangement made to receive the complaints on telephone. Complaints may also be faxed to the Ombudsman.

v. In the case of death of the original complainant, his legal heir can peruse the matter already pending in the ombudsman's office. Similarly the legal heir in respect of a matter that had aggrieved the deceased can also lodge the complaint in person and the cause of complaint continues even after his death.

3- TIME LIMIT

Time limit needs to be set for each stage of the complaint handling process. Time limit may also be clearly defined for acknowledgment of the complaint, admittance of the complaint and submission of comments/reports by the agency concerned and if possible preferably for the completion of investigation and implementation of the recommendation/decision.

4- ACTION WARRANTING NATURE OF COMPLAINTS

Chapter VIII

Complaints against the government functionaries constitute very minor matters to grievances of great magnitude and in most cases all are admitted for investigation. Sometimes there are typical complaints involving more than one agency. Some complaints identify extreme highhandedness and abuse of power on the part of the Agency. The complainant expects a sympathetic approach to his problem and a sincere effort on the part of the investigating officer to resolve and provide some way of assuaging to him. The complainants look to the Ombudsman for something concrete to serve as a solace to them.

CHAPTER 9

IMPLEMENTATION OF THE RECOMMENDATIONS

Chapter IX

Chapter IX

IMPLEMENTATION OF THE RECOMMENDATIONS

(1) MISCONCEPTION ABOUT THE RECOMMENDATION

i) The concept of Ombudsman which is almost universally acknowledged, has also fast adopted by most of the developed and developing countries. Its growth during the last two decades is nothing short of a miracle. As reported in the Directory of Ombudsman and other complaint Handlers issued by the International Institute of Ombudsman in October, 1987,41 countries had Ombudsman and 161 persons were listed as Ombudsman/Deputy Ombudsman. Majority of these countries have a parliamentary form of government and a good number of Asian countries had; appointed Ombudsman/Complaint handlers both at the country and Regional levels in view of the system' utility and usefulness as an effective institution of administrative accountability. This number has fast increased by now. The International Ombudsman Institute consists of Ombudsman of more than 87 countries of the world. Despite the fact that more than 60% of the population of the world is benefited with this system, yet the misconception about the efficacy and impact of Ombudsman's recommendation (popularly known as "Decision") continues unabated.

ii) To dispel the fear and false conception in many minds that Ombudsman is some kind of super-administrator who has power to over rule the decisions of officials, (ministers inclusive) or he is a 'fault finder' with the prime objective to secure punitive action against the defaulting Agency, It has also removed the erroneous impression that the system would turn the flood light of publicity upon the inner working of the administration in various ministries and autonomous bodies. In fact as against the institutions like Anti- Corruption Department, F.I.A, vigilance committees etc., it is observed that Ombudsman all over the world, work with a far less injurious publicity.

iii) Undoubtedly every fair and harmonious community expects protection and respect to its rights from its state functionaries. As the expectations are not fulfilled from the administration (Bureaucracy), the objective is now achieved; through the media of Ombudsman. The statute in addition to the powers of investigations on individual complaints has also conferred on the Ombudsman powers to take up the investigation on his own volition. But it is very often questioned, if the statute has also armed the Ombudsman with necessary powers to ensure that his recommendations and directives are implemented by the concerned agencies and in the event of its defiance or non-compliance inflict necessary punishment.

(2) APPROACH OF "COMAC HONG KONG" ON THE IMPLEMENTATION OF THE RECOMMENDATIONS.

The maxim that "Do it yourself the good governance" is true only in the advanced sophisticated and disciplined societies and this is clearly reflected from the experience whenever expressed by the Ombudsman of those countries on various occasions. For these reasons the Commissioner for Administration and Complaints (COMAC) Hong Kong firmly believed that "Act justly and there will be justice and there will be justice; Act with integrity and there and there will be respect". He experienced no problem in the implementations of his findings though termed as "Recommendations". In his paper, which he read in the Asian Ombudsmen Conference held in Macao May 1996, he stated.

"Referring to the recommendations made, I would like to say that I do not have the power to make legally binding decision. Some would take this as structural flaw in the COMAC system. The COMAC has no real teeth to compel compliance. I cannot agree with this perception, in an open community such as ours, it is always wise to adopt a flexible and pragmatic approach in working out solutions to our problems. The remedial measure. I hope to bring about, is improvements in the public administration through my persuasive power instead of fighting those who might challenge my decision in court. In accordance with the COMAC Ordinance, I can also submit a report to the Governor who will lay the report before the legislative council for consideration. Further more, three months after my annual report, the Chief Secretary will inform the legislative council in the form of a government minute as to whether COMAC's recommendations have been adequately implemented. As such, I can influence those who have the power to review and change decision, which appear to be un-reasonable and oppressive. I would like to reiterate that I am not trying to look for culprits in my investigation. I am trying to look for solutions and I am providing the organization concerned with an independent opinion on the fairness of its administrative procedures. Though fault finding has its place, yet constructive action is the best and most lasting response to the shortcomings in the public administration. This is a belief I have always held and as a matter of fact, all my recommendation and initiatives in the past two years are based on this conviction"

(3) PARLIAMENT AS A REAL SOURCE O STRENGTH IN EUROPEAN COUNTRIES

i) In Denmark, as conceived in Section 3 of the "Directives", the Ombudsmen is obliged to keep himself informed as to whether any person under his jurisdiction pursues unlawful ends, makes arbitrary or unreasonable decisions, or otherwise commits mistakes or acts of negligence in the discharge of his duties. This rule has given the Ombudsmen a very free hand and has opened vide possibilities.

ii) In fact in most of the European countries, Newzealand and in the Far East, the real source of Ombudsmen's authority and strength is parliament and very rarely any government agency will opt that its failure to carry out the recommendation of the Ombudsmen should be discussed or examined by the parliament.

iii) In Finland, the Ombudsmen is; regarded as "guardian of law" and accordingly even if a cabinet member acts in a manner contrary to the law, it is incumbent upon the chancellor of justice to make a representation and if no heed is taken of the representation, the chancellor of justice to make a representation and if no heed is taken of the representation, the chancellor must have his opinion recorded in the minutes of the council of state. He also has the right no ground for prosecution against the member of the cabinet, the chancellor ultimately reports on the case to the parliament.

iv) Perhaps in the context of Pakistan's social political scenario, the Wafaqi Mohtasib of Pakistan was too optimistic of the responsive attitude of the Pakistan bureaucracy, which during the last two decades has fast degenerated and its corruption has touched; the heights. The bureaucracy has no "demeanor of a public servant" and behaves only as a "Government Servant" responsible to follow blindly the instructions and wishes of a party in power and thus seek; rapid corporal gains and promotions. Though in Pakistan, the concept of Swedish Ombudsman has been borrowed and his findings given the name and status of "Recommendation", but to render the system bear purposeful result, the Government did not provide the necessary machinery which may compel and exercise moral and administrative pressure on the defaulting agency either to explain to the satisfaction of the Ombudsman the real constraints preventing the Agency from complying the order/ decision or in the alternative implement the same without any hassle.

v) In the Western Countries as well as in some Far East Countries, the Ombudsman has proved a potent and versatile quasi-judicial weapon to enforce administrative discipline. The parliament is at the back of his recommendations. The power to voice his opinion enables the Parliamentary Commissioner (Ombudsman) to exercise a grinding influence on the administration and provide him with a legal basis for further action. The 'bureaucracy' manning the agencies are spokesman of the rules, where as the 'Ombudsman' is the 'Protector" of the citizen at large.

vi) Mr.Walter Gellhorn has very aptly remarked that "expectations about what Ombudsman can accomplish are too greatly inflated then genuine accomplishments may be forgotten when the inflat4ed expectations explode". It is an admitted position that "an Ombudsman requires no legal powers except powers of enquiry. He is in no sense a court of appeal and hence cannot alter or reverse any government decision. His effectiveness derives entirely from his power to focus public and parliamentary attention upon citizen's grievances" Surely publicity based on impartial inquiry is a powerful liver".

(4) COMPLAINANT'S DISAPPOINTMENT ON NON-IMPLEMENTATION OF RECOMMENDATIONS

i) This disappointment in this regard incidentally has not left any favorable impression about the system amongst the complainants, though the Ombudsman system has gained tremendous popularity in other countries of the world as one of the most rapid, cheap and workable, mechanism for administrative accountability.

ii) It may however be summarized that the bureaucracy seems to have hardened itself with an effusion of negates galore. The attitude has got to be changed. The administration is to be freed from the cobwebs of the cobwebs of the rules and procedure.

The officers in the ministries/ departments should give up their tendency of sharpening their wits on the case till such time either the one takes his hands off his matter in frustration or finds extra procedural methods to get his work done.

iii) As far as the institution of Ombudsman is concerned, the lack of understanding of the nature and extent of the Ombudsman‘s statutory role is regrettable. There is expectation gap, which is damaging. It is widening since the unimplemented decisions are accumulating and the Agencies unwarrantedly invoke appellate powers under Article 32 of the Ombudsman Law as a sheer resort to dilatory tactics.

CHAPTER 10

INTERACTION WITH MEDIA

Chapter X

Chapter X

Interaction with Media

Media is universally recognized as a great power to persuade the government to go along with popular public sentiments.

The need for a close relationship with the press become all the more important when looked in the wake of such ground realities that Ombudsmen has no powers to annual the administrative actions, but when his findings are picked up by the press adds manifold the pressure and persuasive power to his recommendations. The Ombudsmen in such a peculiar situation carves and treads his own path carefully maintaining his independence both of executive and judiciary. This is how he is able to build up a tradition of strong and impartial criticism of government administration besides his role as a "protector of the people".

1- PUBLIC AWARENESS

Admittedly the public awareness of the Office of the Ombudsmen and its functions is the key of success of this institution. Because of illiteracy, unawareness and fear of bureaucracy, the people in Pakistan at large at large have become fatalist and silently bear the perpetuation of the injustice least knowing that there is a door, which if knocked, will give sympathetic response.

The U.K's Parliamentary Commissioners (Ombudsmen) have adopted a variety of methods to ensure public awareness. These are 'press' radio, television, interviews, accepting invitations to address universities, schools, clubs, societies, and local "multiplier" such as citizens Advice Bureau, distributions of posters, and information leaflets. These methods are used in an effort to make the existence and activities of the office of the Ombudsmen better known to potential complainants. The adoption of the Ombudsmen in Pakistan is equally important to publicize the usefulness of this institution and promote good governance. The Ombudsmen's law does not come in the way and he can scrupulously follow these measures with modification and variation as required looking to the psyche of our society and the present level of ethics of journalism.

2- RELATIONSHIP WITH PRESS AND ELECTRONIC MEDIA

The other most effective form of publicity of the creative works of the Ombudsmen is the publicity of the decisions and reports of the "specific studies and investigations" in the national newspapers, including electronic media. Such publicity will constantly keep the Ombudsmen in public eye. Even the government institutions (Agencies) should also help publicize his works.

In Denmark, the Ombudsmen who have been held in high esteem is much popular because of his cordial relations beyond belief with the journalists. His extremely "friendly attitude with the Press" has had the extensive newspaper coverage of his decisions and reports. Press had admired the clarity and well argued decisions of the Ombudsmen and therefore felt no hesitation in attributing the same to them by name. This identifies the Ombudsmen in the public consciousness as a noble "Righter of wrongs". His press releases have been uninflamatory since " in generality the Ombudsmen has dealt with the problems and not with the people".

Professor Ceoferry Sawer of the law department of Australian National University in his famous book "Ombudsmen", has given and interesting account as to how the Swedish press enjoys the liberty and extent of co-operation, unheard in Pakistan and India. In the case of Swedish Ombudsmen. "The Swedish press plays a dominant part in the publicity of the Ombudsmen's work resulting in stimulating his activities and creating impact on the administration. "Editorial exhortations bring issues to his notice for suitable actions. Even the tips from journalists provide him lead to initiate enquiries. More frequently newspaper stories written without the Ombudsmen in mind, suggest to his practiced eye the possibility of discovering "news behind the news". Just as the press makes business for the Ombudsmen so to does he make business for the press. The sweeping principle of Swedish law that the public files should be open to the public indiscriminately means among other things that complaints made to the Ombudsmen can be read by the journalists as can his subsequent correspondences with officials, their explanations and excuses, many of the documentary material that bear on the cases and of course the report of the Ombudsmen's own actions". A reporter for the Swedish News Association visits the Ombudsmen's office every day to examine the incoming mail.

The Swedish Ombudsmen taking note of the official's dissatisfaction had publicly suggested in 1961, that the civil servants organizations and the newspaper publishers associations should negotiate and agreement concerning press coverage.

However unlike Sweden and Denmark where the press has assumed an integral link and close association with the Ombudsmen system and has been engaged in covering extensively the activities of the Ombudsmen, the Norwegian newsmen, on the contrary, had paid little attention to the Ombudsmen. In fact it all depends upon the Ombudsmen's attitude and judgment if the believes more on his relationship with the administration far more important than press. In Pakistan the relationship with the press is incidentally kept in low key. Perhaps this needs a review as press can prove good weaponry in the armory of the Ombudsmen. The print media since recently in very skillfully and in a guarded manner is used by the Provincial Ombudsmen Sindh.

Unfortunately like other countries of the third world, in Pakistan too the telecommunication and electronic media in particular are under strict government control. Ombudsmen here can not use the powerful media on the pattern and in the manner it is utilized in Sweden and Denmark as the concept of free flow of information has not yet taken firm roots in Pakistan, The soil here is contaminated with personality cult and information is kept as a guarded secret under; the plea of administrative exigency.

Chapter X

CHAPTER 11

OMBUDSMEN'S INSTITUTION IN PAKISTAN

Chapter XI

Chapter XI

The idea of Establishment the institutions of Ombudsman in Pakistan found its first expression in the interim Constitution, 1972, providing for appointment of an Ombudsman both at the Federal and Provincial levels. Item 13 of the Federal Legislative list of the Constitution of 1973 provides for the appointment of Federal Ombudsman creating an opportunity appointment of more than one Ombudsman at the Federal level. Similarly, the provincial Legislatures can legislate to appointment Ombudsmen in the Provinces in exercise of residual power under clause (c) of Article 142 of the Constitution.

I- The Establishment of the Wafaqi Mohtasib

The institution of Federal Ombudsman introduced under the name of Wafaqi Mohtasib through this Establishment of this Office of Wafaqi Mohtasib (Ombudsman) order, 1983 Mr. Justice Sardar Muhammad Iqbal was appointed as first Federal Ombudsman of Pakistan.

MOHTASIB' (OMBUDSMAN) SECRETARIAT IN PAKISTAN

As conceived in the Act, all administrative powers are vested in the Ombudsman unless so delegated by him to the Secretary/member administration that normally heads the administrative section of his Secretariat. However like other countries, the Ombudsman's Secretariat is not heavily staffed and instead comprises of only bare essential staff. Amongst the cadre of the officers, the investigating officers normally designated as Director general/ Advisor and Director/ Consultant are the back bone of the Secretariat, whereas the stenographers and steno typist constitute main supporting staff.

The headquarters of the Wafaqi Mohtasib (Ombudsman)'s Secretariat is located at a central place at Islamabad whereas the offices of the Provincial Ombudsman (Punjab, Sindh) are located at the Provincial headquarters viz.: Lahore, Karachi and Muzaffarabad in Azad Jammu & Kashmir. The Regional Offices of the Wafaqi (Federal) Mohtasib are also located at the Provincial Headquarters. The Regional office of Ombudsman Sindh to receive and investigate complaints of upper Sindh is located at Sukkar (Sind).

(a) PERSONNEL STRENGTH OF THE WAFAQI MOHTASIB

There are 50 investigating officers posted at Islamabad and Regional headquarters that deal with the complaints and all such enquiries, which are referred to Ombudsman by the Supreme Court of Pakistan or by the President of Pakistan. The strength in various Secretariats and regional offices varies slightly but is contained within the budget provision. The pattern of the staff reflects following break up:

WAFAQI MOHTASIB

Name of Office

Headquarters (Islamabad)

Regional Office Lahore

Regional Office Karachi

Regional Office Peshawar

Regional Office Quetta

Regional Office Sukkur

Regional Office Multan

Regional Office Faisalabad

Regional Office D.I Khan

Regional Office Gilgut (The office has yet not stared)

(b) **ADMINISTRATION**

Article 3(3) of the President's Order No.1 of 1983 lays down that the Mohtasib shall function independently of the executive and all executive authorities throughout Pakistan are to act in aid of the Mohtasib (Ombudsman). Some officers are also drawn from the serving incumbents in the government and the Establishment Division in consultation with the Mohtasib posts them. The Mohtasib and the Provincial Ombudsman have powers under Article 20 of the Presidential Order or Provincial

Acts to appoint Advisor/Consultant and other ministerial staff. The bare essential staff deals with the huge volume of investigation work and as such each one of them is substantially loaded.

As regards financial powers, till the year 1997-8, re-appropriation of an amount exceeding Rs.50, 000/-from one head to another within budget, required concurrence of the Finance Division. Re-appropriation powers in the provinces are also retained by the Finance Department of the provinces. This had/has caused quite a problem and delay. However with effect from the financial year 1998-99, the situation has been improved. Now the Federal Ombudsman up to an amount of Rs.0.5 can exercise powers of re-appropriation from one head to another head million at a time.

The Ombudsman at the centre and provinces paradoxically do not enjoy full financial powers in respect of their approved budget. This apparently looks awkward and embarrassing that the operation of the Ombudsman's budget is regulated and controlled by the Finance Division/Finance Department though being a government agency these institutions lie under the jurisdiction of the Ombudsman and their acts of mal-administration if any, are investigated by him. In fact Ombudsman should have all financial powers of appropriation and operation of his budget once the same has been cleared/ approved by the National or Provincial Assemblies concerned. To quote an example, to the great embarrassment of the Wafaqi

Mohtasib, for the last three years i.e. since 1996-97 the Finance Division had withheld budget allocation for the purchase of durable goods including vehicles and all types of machinery, and equipment e.g. computer, typewriters, photocopiers etc. The Finance Division as a matter of procedure gives specific clearance and funds for the purchase of these items on case-to-case basis. The position is not much different in provinces. This not only consumes considerable time, but even adversely affects the efficient working of the offices of the Ombudsman.

II- Establishment of the Provincial Ombudsmen Sindh

Mr. S.M Waseem was notified on 12th June 1991 as first Sindh Provincial Ombudsman. He took oath of his office on 18-06-1991.

III- Establishment of the Ombudsmen of Jammu & Azad Kashmir

This Institution was established in 1992 in pursuance of the Azad Jammu & Kashmir's presidential orders 16-08-1991.

IV- Establishment of the Provincial Ombudsmen Pinjab

The Office of Punjab Ombudsman came into existence on 30th September 1996, through Punjab Ordinance No. XI of 1996 with the objective to protect the right of peoples. Mr. Justice Muhammad Munir Khan was appointed as first provincial Ombudsman of Punjab on 29th October 1996.

V- Status Quo Position in the provinces of NWFP& Balochistan

Both NWFP & Baloshistan provinces have not so far appointed the provincial Ombudsman not because there has been no public clamors for some arraignments of administrative accountability. The Federal Ombudsman as indicate in his annual report 1998, was however quite hope full for early setting up of these institutions in these remaining to complete the Ombudsman system in the country.

VI- Establishment of the office of the Federal Tax Ombudsmen

On 11th August 2000 the Institution of the office of Federal Tax Ombudsman under the name The "Establishment of the Office of Federal Tax Ombudsman Ordinance (Ordinance XXXV of 2000), called the Ordinance was promulgated by the Government of Pakistan. Mr. Justice Saleem

Chapter XI

Akhtar was appointed as first Federal Tax Ombudsman of Pakistan.

Concept of the Jurisdiction of the Ombudsman of Pakistan

1- Concept of Cognizance of Ombudsman

i) To balance the interests of the general public against the physical and financial limitations of the government and the judiciary so as to gain a "quick" and "through" judgment to their dispute without being constrained by "Delaying procedures" is and ideal which every legal system strives for. To facilitate this objective a Jude in a manner towards resolving the dispute not to create further hindrances thereon should interpret any procedure adopted in the judicial process.

ii) Franz Kafka in the Trial enlightening the icon of the human predicament that avoid the edge of the nightmare tells the story of a man who is being tried for an undetermined offence and therein clarifies the contradictions that in any legal system:

"it was in the general interest, on the one hand, that the case should be quickly concluded, but on the other hand the interrogations must be through in every respect, although because of the strain involved they must never last too long.

iii) The last fifty six years of Pakistan's existence have witnessed the rapid growth of the public sector which has unfortunately seen a remarkable amount of corruption, delay, incompetence and arbitrary actions being displayed by public officials at all levels in our society. The entire expenses for such corruption, delay, incompetence and arbitrary actions have been borne by the general tax-paying public with little or no "quick" or "through" relief being available to such people.

iv) Consecutive government's responses in relation to such actions have been to bring out specialized laws to deal with corruption.3 The philosophy of both the act were based on the theories of avoidance and concentrated on the recovery of ill gotten wealth as opposed to actually concentrating on systemic corruption in individual departments of the government so as to prevent public official from amassing ill-gotten wealth in the first place. The former amounts to simply a transfer of funds from corrupt public officials to the national exchequer with hardly and amount trickling down for the benefit of the general tax-paying public whose income has illegally been siphoned off in the first place. Quite clearly trying to prevent such payments to be made by the general tax paying public-to-public officials in the world provide more relief.

v) Realizing the incredible financial and sociological impact of such actions by public official, highlighted by public official administering tax laws, the present government adopted a sensible "micro" approach to the problem attacking the problem at its root and promulgated the Establishment of the Office of the Federal Tax Ombudsman Ordinance, 20005 (EFTO) to:

> "Diagnose, investigate, redress and rectify any injustice done to person through misadministration by functionaries administering tax laws"

vi) Gregory and Pearson submit that it. ....was not unreasonable to argue that complainants should have been given direct access to the commissioner ,instead of being required to ask MP's to referee their cases to the Office or that his jurisdiction was too restricted, in the sense that the office was empowered to investigate only administrative action taken by central govt. departments, and not even all of that or that the inclusion of the term misadministration in the parliamentary commissioner act, 1967 has been ill considered because it has both unduly restricted the range and number of complaints open to unduly the grounds on which he was authorized to criticize departmental action subject to complain.

2- Reasons to initiate the institution of Ombudsman in Pakistan

i) Pakistan has attempted to learn from the experiences of other countries while developing its own Ombudsman offices. At present five different Ombudsmen is operation in Pakistan. The Wafaqi MohatasibThe Ombudsman Sindh, The Ombudsman Punjab. The Ombudsman Balochistan and the Federal Tax Ombudsman. It is generally considered that the effectiveness and competence of the first fourth of these offices have been dwarfed by the work that the

Federal Tax Ombudsman has completed in the last three years.

3- Cognizance by the EFTO

i) The federal Tax Ombudsman has been incredibly effective in dealing with the complaints made to him. Until the end of the year 2004, 6094 complaints have been instituted with the Federal Tax Ombudsman out of which 5760 have been decided. However due to bad drafting of the enabling statute, similar issues that were clarified by Gregory and Pearson above regarding the jurisdiction of the Ombudsman and the definition of misadministration have raised their head in this jurisdiction.

(A) The Federal Tax Ombudsman as per subsection (1) of section 9 of the EFTO

"May on a complaint by any aggrieved person, or on a reference by the president, the senate or the national Assembly, as the case may be or on a motion of the Supreme Court or a high court made during the course of any proceedings before it or of this own motion, investigate any allegation of misadministration on the part of the Revenue Division or any Tax Employee.

ii) Complaints can therefore only be invited by the Federal Tax Ombudsman in relation to acts amounting to Misadministration against the Revenue Division itself or against any individual Tax Employee.

iii) Misadministration is defined by sub-section (3) of Section 2 of the EFTO which.

"Includes"

(i) Is decision, process recommendation, act of omission or commission which.

a. Is contrary to law, rules or regulations or is a departure from established practice or procedure, unless it is bona fide and for valid reasons.
b. Is perverse, arbitrary or unreasonable, unjust, biased, oppressive, or discriminatory.
c. Is based on irrelevant ground or
d. Involves the exercise of powers, or the failure or refusal to do so, for corrupt or improper motives, such as bribery, jobbery, favoritism, nepotism, and administrative excesses;

ii. neglect, inattention, delay, incompetence, inefficiency and ineptitude, in the administration or discharge of duties and responsibilities.

iii. Repeated notices, unnecessary attendance , or prolonged hearings while deciding cases involving.

   a. Assessment of income or wealth;
   b. Determination of liability of tax or duty
   c. Classification or valuation of goods.
   d. Settlement of claims of refund, rebate or duty drawback; or
   e. Determination of fiscal and tax concessions or exemptions.

iv. Willful errors in the determination of refunds, rebates or duty drawbacks

v. Deliberate withholding or nonpayment of refunds, rebates or duty drawbacks already determined by the competent authority.

vi. Coercive methods of tax recovery in cases where default in payment of tax or duty is not apparent from record; and

vii. Avoidance of disciplinary action against an officer or official whose order of assessment or valuation is held by a competent appellate authority to be vindictive, capricious, biased or patently illegal."

vi) Lord Watson in Dilworth vs. Commissioner for Stamps observed.

"The word "include is very generally used in interpretation clauses in order to enlarge the meaning of the words or phrases occurring innate body of the statutes; and when it is so used these words or phrases must be construed or comprehending, not only such things as theory signify according to their natural import, but also things which the interpretation clause declares that they shall include. But the word include is susceptible of another construction, which may become imperative if the context of the act is sufficient to show that it was not merely employed for the purpose of adding to the natural significance of the words or expression defined. It may be equivalent to "mean and include "and in that case it may afford an exhaustive explanation the meaning which for the purposes of the act, my invariably be attached to the words or expressions."

v) The dicta of Lord Watson in Dilworth vs. Commissioner for land and Income tax ahs been accepted and applied by the Supreme Court of Pakistan in Mushtaq Ahmad vs. The State and in Don Basco High School vs. The assistant Director. In Usmania Glass Sheet Factory

Limited, Chittagong vs. Sales Tax Officer, Chittagong although no specific reference was made to Lord Watson's Judgment, the first sentence is clearly reproduced therein.

Vi) As per the judgment of Lord Watson, the word includes can have two separate connotations each of which depends on the purpose of the Act in question. It may be construed so as not to be exhaustive i.e. to go beyond the specific definition given to the word being defined in the Act, whereby actions which can be attributed to the natural definition of that word are also to be considered as being within the scope of the Act. Alternatively a more restrictive approach may be employed where the definition in the Act is considered to be exhaustive if it is possible to show that the intention of the Act was simply to restrict the scoop of the Act to the specified acts.

vii) Nothing within the Act itself could be construed so as to limit the definition of the world misadministration to the definition of the world misadministration to the actions defined in sub-clause (3) of section 2 of the EFTO. Further looking at the preamble of the EFTO clarifying the purpose and intent of the Act to:

"Diagnose, investigate, redress and rectify any injustice done to a person through misadministration by functionaries administering tax laws. It is clear that a non exhaustive approach should be adopted in the interpretation of the word "Misadministration" Therefore on a complaint being made by a person with locus standi any other action which may fall within the natural definition of the word "misadministration" attributable to the "Revenue Division" or a "Tax

Employee" should also be included within the ambit of actions that the federal Tax Ombudsman is able to redress in exercise of his Jurisdiction under the EFTO.

4- Bar of Jurisdiction is Ousted

i) Sub-Section (2) of Section 9 of the EFTO clarifies that:

"The federal Ta Ombudsman shall not have jurisdiction to investigate or inquire into matters which.

a. are sub-justice before a court of competent jurisdiction or tribunal or broad or authority on the date of the receipt of a complain, reference or motion by him. or

b. relate to assessment of income or wealth, determination of liability of tax or duty, interpretation of law, rules and regulations relating to such assessment, determination classification or valuation in respect of which legal remedies of appeal, review of revision are available under the Relevant Legislation."

ii) Where the issue of misadministration is sub-judice before a court, tribunal, board or authority of competent jurisdiction at the time of the filing of the complaint the Federal Tax Ombudsman has clarified that in such circumstances he will not have jurisdiction to entertain the complaint. In contrast where there is a matter being heard at the time of the filing of the complaint between the same complainant and the Revenue Division/Tax Employee which does not raise the issues of misadministration; so as to fill the lacunae created, the federal tax Ombudsman has considered that the issue of misadministration not being sub-judice that he has jurisdiction to entertain the complaint.

iii) Where a submission has been made that a case has been filed prior to the filing of the complaint the Federal Tax Ombudsman has clarified that in such circumstances he will not have jurisdiction to entertain the complaint. In contrast where there is a matter being heard at the time of the filing of the complaint between the same complainant and the Revenue Division/Tax Employee which does not raise the issues of misadministration; so as to fill lacunae created, the Federal Tax Ombudsman has considered that the issue of misadministration not being sub-judice that he has jurisdiction to entertain the complaint. Where a submission has been made that a case has been filed prior to the filing of the complaint and the issue f misadministration raised in the complaint is Sub-judice, the onus will be on the person making the submission to satisfy the federal tax

Ombudsman that the issue of misadministration has in fact been raised in another forum of competent jurisdiction prior to the filing of the complaint. Failure to produce evidence to such effect would raise a presumption that the matter was not sub-judice allowing the Federal Tax Ombudsman to exercise jurisdiction to entertain the complaint. Correspondingly where the complainant had field an action and subsequently withdrawn the same and a certified copy of the order had been provided by the complainant satisfying the Federal Tax Ombudsman that the matter was no longer sub judice jurisdiction would be considered to have vested in the Federal Tax Ombudsman to entertain the complaint.

iv) In unreported cases the Revenue Division have attempted to argue that if the matter is before a Board e.g. the Board of Revenue in whatever capacity, then under clause (a) of sub-section (2) of section 9 of the EFTO, jurisdiction of the Federal tax Ombudsman would be ousted. Such arguments are clearly misconceived in light of the ejusdem generis principle of statutory interpretation.

Lord Campbell in outlined the principle R vs. Edmondson.

"..........where there are general words following particular and specific words, the general words must be confined to things of the same kind as those specified."

v) The principle has recently been applied in the Supreme Court of Pakistan in Jammat-iIslami Pakistan vs. Federation of Pakistan. Whereby Mr. Justice Irshad Hasan Khan (as he was then) clarified. "The doctrine of ejusdem generic is well settled it meant that where general words follow an enumeration of persons or things by person or things, bywords of a particular meaning such general words are not to be construed in their widest extent but are to held as applying only to persons or things of the same general kind of class as those specifically mentioned."

vi) The words Board or Authority following the words court or tribunal in clause (a) of sub-section (2) of section 9 of the EFTO would be referring to a Board or Authority exercising judicial functions as opposed to any board or authority exercising administrative, procedural or any other function; there latter being excluded from the purview of the exclusion clause thereby granting jurisdiction of the Federal tax Ombudsman to entertain such a complaint.

i. Matters relating to assessment of income at al.

The federal Tax Ombudsman when interpreting clause (b)

of sub-section (2) of Section 9 of the EFTO clarifies that any acts of maladministration by the Revenue Division or a Tax Employee are acts independent of the actions listed in clause (b) of sub-section (2) of section 9 of the EFTO. Such acts of maladministration thereby not coming with the within the purview of the exclusion clause can be entertained by the Federal tax Ombudsman.

vii) Such a view was however not acceptable to the Revenue Division or the Tax Employees who would time and again object the jurisdiction of the Federal Tax Ombudsman. Exasperated, the Federal tax

Ombudsman vents his frustration with the Revenue Division in Moderan Baby Cycle Store vs. Secretary, Revenue Division, Islamabad where he stated. "In its reply Department has raised usual objection to the jurisdiction. It has time and again been ruled and explained that in cases where maladministration has been alleged independent of the controversy in the matter, the fact that remedy under the statute has been provided will not be a bar to jurisdiction of the Federal Tax Ombudsman to investigate into the allegation of maladministration. The Federal tax Ombudsman can investigate into allegations of maladministration without enquiring into the merits of the case."

5- The Federal Tax Ombudsman Further Clarifies.

i) "It is true that the Establishment of the Office of the Federal Tax Ombudsman Ordinance, 2000 has defined the term maladministration and the jurisdiction of the Federal Tax Ombudsman is to investigate and make recommendation as provided under the Ordinance. Therefore, where maladministration is alleged and established the Federal tax Ombudsman shall be within his jurisdiction to give his recommendation and finding which may even affect the merits of the cases.

ii) The federal Tax Ombudsman gains inspiration from adopting a purposive approach to interpret such legislation. Parke B. In Becker and Smith. "It is a very useful ruled in the constructional a statute to adhere to the ordinary meaning of a statute to adhere to the ordinary meaning of the words used, and to the grammatical construction, unless tat is at variance with the intention of the legislature to be collected from the statute itself or leads to any manifest absurdity or repugnance. In which case the language may be varied or modified to avoid such inconvenience but not further."

iii) Further inspiration may be obtained from the dicta of Mr. Justice Faze Akbar in Pakistan Tabacco Company Limited vs. Pakistan Tobacco Company Employees Union, Dacca approves the passage from Maxwell's Book on Interpretation of Statute sheering he quotes.

"It is a cardinal rule of interpretation that when the language used by the Legislature admits of two constructions the Court should no adopt a construction which would lead to an absurdity or obvious injustice but should adopt that construction which appears to be most in accord with reason and justice.

The preamble of the EFTO clarifies that the Federal Tax Ombudsman is to:
"Diagnose, investigate, redress and rectify any injustice done to a person through misadministration by functionaries administering." Sub-Section (2) of the Section 9 of the EFTO is in direct variance with the intention of the legislature as expressed in the preamble and in fact defeats the intention of the legislature as indicated therein. Any interpretation as to the provisions of the jurisdiction of the EFTO must be considered so as to avoid repugnancy, absurdity or injustice and should be in accord with reason and justice.

7- The doctrine of Ultra vires

i) The doctrine of Ultra vires captures the idea that any action of the public official must be exercised within the jurisdiction conferred on that public official by its enabling act. Any actions e.g. arbitrary decision, acts of misadministration, etc. would be considered to be outside the jurisdiction conferred on the public official by the enabling act and be considered ultra vires and void.

ii) Chief Justice Muhammad Haleem in the Supreme Court of Pakistan in Utility Stores Corporation of Pakistan Limited vs. Punjab Labour Appellate Tribuna has clarified the doctrine:

"It is not right to say that the Tribunal, which invested with the jurisdiction to decide a particular mater, has the jurisdiction to decide it, "rightly or wrongly" because the condition of the grant of jurisdiction is that it should decide the matter in accordance with the law. When the Tribunal goes wrong in law, it goes outside the jurisdiction conferred on it because the Tribunal has the jurisdiction to decide rightly but not the jurisdiction to decide wrongly. Accordingly, when the tribunal makes an error of law in deciding the matter before it, it goes outside the jurisdiction and, therefore, a determination of the Tribunal which is shown to be erroneous on a point of law can be quashed....on the ground that it is in excess of jurisdiction."

iii) Any acts of Misadministration as defined in the EFTO including but not limited to acts of misadministration amounting to violations of the rules of natural justice would be acts that are outside the scope of the jurisdiction conferred on the Revenue Division or the Tax Employee an error of law and liable to be declared a void and quashed.

iv) Such "misadministration" assessments of income or wealth, determination of liability of tax or duty, classification or valuation of goods, interpretation of law, rules and regulations relating to such assessment, determination classification or valuation are not capable of being covered with the definition of such words as defined in their enabling statute. Clearly such acts are mis-assessments of income or wealth, mis-determinations of liability of tax or duty, mis-classification or valuation of goods, Mis-interpretation of law, rules and regulations relating to such assessment, mis-determination mis-classification or mis-valuation and cannot be considered to be acts made within the jurisdiction conferred by their enabling acts.

v) Where such misadministration has occurred the Federal Tax Ombudsman is clearly within his jurisdiction to consider such acts of the Revenue Division or Tax

Employees as being independent acts that are ultra vires of the jurisdiction conferred thereon are liabel to be entertained by the Federal Tax Ombudsman.

vi) An alternative approach may be considered in the interpretation of clause (b) of Sub-section (2) of Section 9 of the EFTO. The Federal Tax Ombudsman shall not have jurisdiction to investigate or inquire into matters which.

(b) Relate to assessment of income or earth, determination of liability of tax or duty, classification or valuation of goods, interpretation of law, rules and regulations relating to such assessment, determination classification or valuation in respect of which legal remedies of appeal, review or revision are available under the Relevant Legislation."

vii) The interpretation of the section by substituting the word" concerning" instead of the word "relate" in the beginning of the clause (b) of sub-section (2) of Section (9) of the EFTO would have the effect of being inclusive thereby clarifying that any actions that are concerned with assessments of income would be outside the jurisdiction of the Federal tax Ombudsman.

viii) Alternative the word by substituting the word" connected" instead of the word "relate" in the beginning of the clause (b) of sub-section (92) of section 9, of the EFTO would have the effect of creating a distinction between an action that was connected with an assessment of income as opposed to the action of the assessment of income itself thereby clarifying that any actions that are concerned with assessments would be within the jurisdiction of the Federal Tax ombudsman.

ix) Matters connected with the assessment of income would be limited to matters that arose prior to the assessment process i.e. the laws, rules and policies established by the Revenue Division or a Tax employee. Al actions connected with the assessment of income etc. would be included within the jurisdiction of the Federal Tax Ombudsman.

x) It is settled ruled of the interpretation of statues that in than case of doubts or contradictions that may be raised in relation to the interpretation of the section of a statue reference may be made to the intention of the legislature as indicated in the preamble of the statute.

In Amiruddin vs. West Punjab Province Mr. Justice Shahabuddin clarifies the principle by stating. " ......when more that one interpretation is possible that construction should be preferred which carries into effect the object of the statue."

xi) The preamble of the EFTO clarifies that the role of the Federal Tax Ombudsman is to:

"diagnose, investigate, redress and rectify any injustice done to a person through misadministration by functionaries administrating tax laws"

xii) Keeping in mind the preamble of the EFTO so as to deal with all matters relating to misadministration and to rectify and injustice done to a person through such misadministration any possible interpretations of the section of the EFTO must be construed in favour of the finding the jurisdiction of the Federal Tax

Ombudsman of deal with such matters as opposed to destroying it. This position may be reinforced by the judgments of Mr. Justice Fasle Akbar, that where two interpretations to a statute are possible the one that the interpretation that leads to the absurdity shluld be avoided and the one which, further reason and justice should be adopted.

xiii) One would hope that the government of the day having created an organization that is effective, realizes that it is in the ling trem interest of the economy and the government to allow the Federal tax Ombudsman to develop further in an attempt to ensure that the tax paying public does not have to add additional costs in terms of kickbacks and Employees.

xiv) It is considered that the solution to the government problem lies in the very success of the effectiveness of the Federal Tax Ombudsman. A few over burdeded competent well-paid individual will provide more for revenue for the state in the long run that a large number of under paid employees ever will.

SLIENT FEATURES OF THE ORDINANCE

The salient features of the Establishment of the Office of Federal Tax Ombudsman Ordinance, 2000 hereinafter referred to as "the Ordinance" are being highlighted hereunder for the benefit of stakeholder.

Constitutional Attributes

Item 13 of the Federal Legislative List

Parliament has the power of enactment, under item 13 of the Federal Legislative List, for the establishment of s many Federal Ombudsmen as the legislative deems necessary.

Expenditure Charged upon Federal Consolidate Fund

Chapter XI

Article 81 of the Constitution provides that the following expenditure would be the expenditure charged upon Federal Consolidated Fund:-

a) The remuneration payable to the President and other Expenditure relating to his office, and the remuneration payable to :-

   i. The Judges of the Supreme Court;
   ii. The Chief Election Commissioner;
   iii. The Chairman and the Deputy Chairman of the Senate;
   iv. The speaker and the Deputy Speaker of the National Assembly;
   v. The Auditor General;

b) The administrative expenses, including the remuneration payable to officers and servants of the Supreme Court, the department of the Auditor General and the Office of the Chief Election Commissioner and of the Election Commission and the Secretariats of the Senate and the National Assembly;

c) All the debt charges for which the Federal Government is liable, including interest, sinking fund charges, the payment of the amortisation of the capital, and other expenditure in connection with the raising of loans, and the service and redemption of debt on the security of the Federal Consolidated Fund;

d) Any sums required to satisfy any judgment, decree or award against Pakistan by any Court or Tribunal; and

e) Any other sums declared by the Constitution or by Act of [Majlis-e-Shoora (Parliament)] to be so charged.

Section 35 of the Establishment of the Office of Federal Tax Ombudsman Ordinance provides that the remuneration payable to Federal Tax Ombudsman and the administrative expenses of the office, including the remuneration payable to eligible staff members, nominees and grantees, shall be an expenditure charged upon the Federal Consolidated fund.

This feature of the Office of Federal Tax Ombudsman warrants special delegation of by the Chief Executive of Pakistan to the Offices and the Institutions enumerated in Article 81 of the Constitution in relaxation of the Finance Division O.M. No. F.3 (4) Exp.III/2000 dated 30.06.2000 for the purpose of his function under section 24 of the Ordinance.

A fixed tenure

The President of Pakistan shall appoint the Federal Tax Ombudsman for tenure of four years.

Independent of Executive

The incumbent shall perform his functions and exercise his powers independent of the executive and all executive authorities throughout Pakistan shall act in aid of the Federal Tax Ombudsman. (Sub-section (3) of section 3)

Public servant

The Federal Tax Ombudsman and staff members, according to section 27 of the Ordinance shall be public servants within the meaning of section 21 of the Pakistan Penal Code (Act XLV of 1860).

Basic Objective

The objective of appointment of Federal Tax Ombudsman, as enumerated in the preamble of the Ordinance, is to diagnose, investigate, redress and rectify any **injustice done to a person through maladministration** of the government functionaries administering tax laws.

The **Division** whose diagnosis and investigation is aimed at has been defined under sub-section (7) of section 2 of the Ordinance as under:-

"The **Revenue Division** means the administrative unit responsible for the conduct of business of the Federal Government in matters relating directly or indirectly with the collection of revenue from the federal taxes, duties, cess or fees and declared as such by the Federal Government, and includes all its subordinate departments, offices and agencies."

Maladministration has been defined to include:

(a) A decision, process, recommendation, act of omission or commission which-

I. is contrary to law, rules or regulations or is a departure from established practice and procedure, unless it is bona fide and for valid reasons.

II. is preserves, arbitrary or unreasonable, unjust, biased, oppressive, or discriminatory;

III. is based on irrelevant grounds; or

IV. involves the exercise of powers, or the failure or refusal to do so, for corrupt or improper motives, such as bribery, jobbery, favouritism, nepotism and administrative excesses;

b. neglect, inattention, delay, incompetence, inefficiency and ineptitude, in the administration or discharge of duties and responsibilities;

c. repeated notices, unnecessary attendance or prolonged hearings while deciding cases involving-

    I. assessment of income or wealth

    II. determination of liability of tax or duty;

    III. classification or valuation of goods;

    IV. settlement of claims of refund, rebate or duty drawbacks; or

    V. Determination of fiscal and tax concessions or exemption.

d. willful errors in the determination of refunds, rebates or duty drawbacks;

e. deliberate withholding or non-payment of refunds, rebates or duty drawbacks already determined by the competent authority;

f. coercive methods of tax recovery in cases where default in payment of tax or duty is not apparent from record; and

g. Avoidance of disciplinary action against an officer or official whose order of assessment or valuation is held by a competent appellate authority to be vindictive, capricious, biased or patently illegal.

<u>Scope of Action</u>

The jurisdiction, functions and powers of the Federal Tax Ombudsman covers following areas:-

Investigation involving any allegation of maladministration on the part of Revenue Division or any tax employee

(i) on a complaint by an aggrieved person

(ii) on a reference by the president,

(iii) on a reference by the Senate

(iv) on a reference by the National Assembly

(v) on a motion of the Supreme Court during the course of any proceedings before

(vi) on a motion of the High Court during the course of

any proceedings before it and

(vii) of his own motion.

However, subsection (2) of section 9 of the Ordinance excludes from the jurisdiction of the Federal Tax Ombudsman:

(i) matters which are subjudice on the date of receipt of a complaint; and

(ii) matters where legal remedies of appeal, review or revision are available which relate to:

Assessment of income or wealth, determination of liability of tax or duty,

Classification or valuation of goods, interoperation of law, rules and regulations relating to such assessment determination, classification or valuation under the Relevant Legislation.

The foregoing provisions of clauses (a) and (b) of sub-section (2) of section 9 restricting the jurisdiction of Federal Tax Ombudsman have caused serious resentment among the trade bodies, Chambers of Commerce and industry Pakistan Tax Bars as they feel that the jurisdiction should be unfettered. Mean while, the Federal Tax Ombudsman, after hearing various parties, has held, in several cases, that notwithstanding the foregoing restrictive provisions, if any allegation of maladministration is made which is not directly under consideration of any authority, court , tribunal or board , federal Tax Ombudsman shall have the Jurisdiction to investigate and decide the issues of maladministration.

Moreover, the service matters of tax employees of the Revenue Division are also excluded from the jurisdiction of Federal Tax Ombudsman.

Filing Procedure

The procedure for filing complaints with the Federal Tax Ombudsman is provided under section 10 of the ordinance. The requirements of sub-section (1) of section 10 are:

i) A written complaint addressed to the Federal Tax Ombudsman on solemn affirmation in writing that contents of the compliant are true and correct.

ii) In case complaint is not verified on solemn affirmation, an affidavit reiterating the contents of complaint should be field.

iii) Complaint or solemn affirmation / affidavit is to be signed by the aggrieved person or, in case of death of the aggrieved person by his legal representative.

iv) Complaint can be delivered in the office of the Federal Tax Ombudsman by hand or by other mean of communication.

Sub-section (2) of the said section provides that anonymous or pseudonymous complaints shall not be entertained. Sub-section (3) places a time bar on the filing of a compliant. The aggrieved party must file a complaint within six moths from the date of receipt compliant. However, the Federal Tax Ombudsman may conduct any investigation pursuant to the compliant which is not in time if he consider that they are special circumstances which he deems proper in the entrust of justice to entertain the compliant.

Where the Federal Tax Ombudsman purposes to conduct an investigation he shall in accordance with sub-section (4) or provide an opportunity to the Secretary of the Revenue Division or to the functionaries whose action is the subject matter of the compliant to reply to the allegations contained therein through a notice and indicate the date when he proposes to conduct an investigation. Further, Sub-section (10) provides for an opportunity to the parties to be heard in person or through an authorized representative by the Federal Tax Ombudsman.

However, in case FTO decides no to conduct an investigation, sub-section (10) provides that he shall send to the complaint a statement of his reasons for not conducting the investigation.

Sub-section (5) provides that normally every investigation shall be conducted in private. However, the Federal Tax Ombudsman may adopt such procedures, as he considers appropriate for such investigation. He my also obtain information from such persons and in such manner and make such inquiries as he thinks fit.

Any person who attends or furnishes information for the purpose of any investigation shall receive, according to the provisions of with sub-section (7), expenses and allowances from the Federal Tax Ombudsman in accordance with the rules made under the Ordinance.

The Federal Tax Ombudsman, in exercise of his powers under sub-section (9), my require any tax employee to furnish any information or product any document which in his opinion is relevant and helpful in the conduct of the investigation and there shall be no obligation to maintain secrecy in respect of disclosure of any information or document for the purpose of such investigation.

Sub-section (8) permits the Revenue Division to take further action in respect of any matter which is subject of investigation. It is, however, clarified that such action should be just, proper and according to law and should not be biased, prejudiced or intended to forestall and frustrate the investigation.

Force of Recommendations

The Federal Tax Ombudsman has the authority to make recommendations under Section 11 within a period of sixty days from the date of receipt of the compliant, reference or motion, as the case may be, if he is of the opinion that the matter considered amounts to maladministration.

If, after conducting n investigation, it appears to the Federal Tax Ombudsman that an injustice has been caused to the person aggrieved in consequence of maladministration and that the injustice has not been or will not be remedied, he may, if he thinks fit, put up a special report on the case before the President.

Where the Federal Tax Ombudsman communicates his finding with recommendations, the Revenue Division shall, within the time specified, inform him about the action taken on his recommendations or the reasons for not complying with the same. If the Revenue Division does not comply with the recommendations of the Federal Tax Ombudsman or does not give reasons to the satisfaction of the Federal Tax Ombudsman for non-compliance, it shall be treated as "Defiance of Recommendation."

The Federal Tax Ombudsman, shall forward a copy of the compliance report or communication received by him from the Revenue Division to the complainant or the President, the Senate, the National Assembly, the Supreme Court or High Court as the case may be.

Chapter XI

Defiance of Recommendations.

It is the duty of the Revenue Division and the tax employees to implement the findings, made under section 11 and 12, within thirty days of communication of such decision to the concerned Tax Employee.

In each instance of defense of recommendations, a report by Federal Tax Ombudsman shall become a part of the personal file or character roll of the tax employee primarily responsible for the defiance. Such tax employee primarily shall also be liable for contempt as provided in section 16.

In case there is defiance of recommendations by a tax employee with regard to their implementation, the Federal Tax Ombudsman may refer the matter to the President who, in his discretion, may direct the Revenue Division to implement the recommendations and inform the Federal Tax Ombudsman accordingly.

The Ordinance provides, under section 13, that the Federal Tax Ombudsman may refer the cases to the Revenue Division for corrective or disciplinary action or both where he is satisfied that the any employee is guilty of the allegations advance against him. The Revenue Division require to report compliance with in 30 days of receipt preference following which the Federal Tax Ombudsman may bring the matter to the notice of the President for such action as he may deem fit. Besides, he may take action for contempt under section 16 as well.

Powers of the Federal Tax Ombudsman

Code of Civil Procedure at FTO`s Call

The Federal Tax Ombudsman shall exercise powers for the purposes of the Ordinance as are vested in a civil court under the Code of Civil Procedure, 1908 (Act V of 1908), in respect of:

i) summoning and enforcing the attendance of any person and examining him on oath,

ii) Compelling the production of documents,

iii) Receiving evidence on affidavit, and

iv) Issuing commission for the examination of witness.

Any person can be required to furnish information of point that relevant of the subject matter of any investigation.

The Federal Tax Ombudsman, or any other person authorized in writing by the Federal Tax Ombudsman in this behalf, may also exercise such power in the course of conducting an investigation under the provisions of the Ordinance.

Protection to Revenue Functionaries against False Allegations

Where the complaints are found to be false, frivolous or vexatious, the Federal Tax Ombudsman may award reasonable compensation to the Revenue Division or tax employee against whom the complaint was made. The amount of such compensation shall be recoverable from the complainant as an arrear of land revenue. However, award of compensation shall not debar the aggrieved person from seeking civil and criminal remedy.

Criminal or Disciplinary Action Against Errant Revenue Functionaries

The Federal Tax Ombudsman may, in addition to taking other actions under this Ordinance, refer the matter to the appropriate authority or taking disciplinary action against the Revenue Division or the tax employee who disregards the orders of the Federal Tax Ombudsman. In case he has reasons to believe that the Tax employee has acted in a manner warranting criminal or disciplinary proceedings against him, he may refer the matter to the appropriate authority for necessary action to be taken within the time specified by him.

Commissioning Staff To Administer Oath / Attestations / Affirmations

The Staff Members and nominees of the Office may be commissioned by the Federal Tax

Ombudsman to administer oath for the purpose of this Ordinance and to attest various affidavits, affirmations or declarations which shall be admitted in evidence in all proceedings under this Ordinance without proof of the signature or seal or official character of such person.

Power of Review

The Federal Tax Ombudsman shall have the power to review ,any finding communicated or recommendations made or any order passed by him under section 14(8) of the Ordinance.

Power to enter and search (Sec 15)

The Federal Tax Ombudsman or any authorized staff member in this behalf may for purpose of making investigation enter any premises if he has reason to believe that any article, books of accounts or any other document relating to the subject matter of investigation may be found and may;

a) Search such premises and inspect any article books of accounts and documents
b) Take extracts or copies of such books of account and documents
c) Impound or seal such articles, books of accounts or documents
d) Make an inventory

All searches shall be carried out in accordance with the provisions of Code of Criminal Procedure 1898 (Act V of 1898)

Power to punish for contempt

Under section 16, the Federal Tax Ombudsman has, mutatis mutandis, the same power to punish for contempt as the Supreme Court of Pakistan has.

Inspection Teams

The Federal Tax Ombudsman may constitute an Inspection Team for performance of any of the functions of the Federal Tax Ombudsman.

Chapter XI

Standing or Advisory Committees

The Federal Tax Ombudsman may, whenever he thinks fir, establish Standing or Advisory Committees at specified places with specified jurisdictions.

Awarding Cost / Compensation

The Federal Tax Ombudsman may award cost or compensation, in accordance with section 22, to an aggrieved party for loss or damage suffered by him on account of maladministration by Tax Employee or the Revenue Division after considering explanation and hearing such Tax Employee or Revenue Division. In cases involving payment of illegal gratification to any Tax Employee or any person on his behalf, or to misappropriation or criminal breach of trust or cheating, the Federal Tax Ombudsman may order the payment thereof for credit to the Government or pass such other order as he may deem fit.

Representation to the President

Representation to the President can be made under section 32 either by Revenue Division or by any person aggrieved by the recommendations of the Federal Tax Ombudsman, with in 30 days of the recommendations, who may pass such orders thereon as he may deem fit.

Informal Resolution of Disputes

A very significant feature of the Ordinance is section 33 which provides for informal resolution of dispute. The authority of Federal Tax Ombudsman to informally conciliate, amicably resolve, stipulate, settle or ameliorate any grievance overrides other provisions of the Ordinance. The Federal Tax Ombudsman can proceed under this provision without requiring any written memorandum and without the necessity of docketing any complaint or issuing any official notes.

The Federal Tax Ombudsman has framed **"Investigation and Disposal of Complaints Regulations"** to regulate the procedure for conduct of business or the exercise of powers under the

Ordinance as provided under sub-section (11) of section 10 of the Ordinance.

Federal Tax Ombudsman can also make Rules under section 36 with the approval of the President for carrying out the purpose of the Ordinance.

Under section 29 no court authority shall have jurisdiction to

i) Question the validity of any action taken, or intended to be taken, or made, or anything done or purporting to have been taken made or done under the Ordinance.

ii) Grant any injunctions or stay, or to make any interim order in relation to any proceeding before, or anything done or intended to be done or purporting to have been done by, or under the Orders or at the instance

Chapter XI

of the Federal Tax Ombudsman.

According to section 37, the provisions of this Ordinance shall have effect notwithstanding anything contrary contained in any other law for the time being in, including the Establishment of the Office of Wafaqi Mohtsib (Ombudsman) Order, 1983 (President's Order No. 1 of 1983.)

Chapter XI

CHAPTER 12

OMBUDSMAN IN ASIAN COUNTRIES

Chapter XII

Chapter XII

OMBUDSMAN IN ASIAN COUNTRIES

The study of the working of some of the Ombudsmen or office holders differently designated as Parliamentary Commissioner, Commissioner for administrative complaints etc. In various Asian countries, will definitely help in understanding this system in this part of the world. In fact each such country has tailored the system as suited to their traditions, psyche, and administrative requirement whereas the philosophy and basic concept of providing relief and protection to the common citizen against the arbitrariness and traumatic approach of the bureaucracy, has remained the same. Since recently 75 countries were enrolled as members of the International Ombudsman Institute besides several Regional Associations of system as existed in Pakistan is studied in a separate chapter. The Ombudsman system which had its origin in Sweden, had in fact radiated and blossomed in quite a good number of Asian Countries as the deteriorating administrative environment in those countries provide a ready and receptive soil for such experiments of remedial measures. Of course the diverse culture, language, and different legal and Government systems have given birth to such institutions vested with jurisdiction and powers not identical to each other, yet they all in their own way and according to their own laws and rules try to redress grievances of their people.

i. CHINA

The Government of China is pursuing its fundamental aim of serving the people and has strived to provide the citizen an honest and accountable administration. The first ever-supervisory Organization known as 'People's Supervisory Commission' was established in October 1949 under the State Government Administration Council. This was abolished due to restructuring of the state administration system. To establish and improve the national supervisory organs and give full play to their role, a separate Ministry of Supervision was re-established in 1987. The Ministry of supervision, under the leadership of the Premier, is the nation's Supreme administrative supervisory body. Its main functions are to supervise the Government Organs and their personnel, according to the laws, regulations and policies, and to see that they perform their official duties honestly, accountably and industriously. The Ombudsman in China has the following main features: -

MAIN FEATURES (POWERS AND JURISDICTION)

- Ombudsman in China is designated as MINISTER FOR SUPERVISION

- He primarily focuses on eradication of Corruption, being the root cause of mal-administration.

- Exercise his functions independently, and is not subject to any interference from other administrative organs, public organizations or individuals.

- He is nominated by the Premier and appointed by the State President with the approval of the National People's Congress. In other words, all concerned with the state who have the powers, authority, and jurisdiction, are participating in his appointment. He is a politburo member of the Communist party, which guarantees political support to the institution of Ombudsman. As a matter of fact, he is a member of the stated Council.

- He is number three in warrant of precedence. This places him on a powerful footing in supervising the working and performance of the Government functionaries.

- He even enjoys powers to look into the conduct of the members of the Federal Cabinet in the discharge of duties towards the public in general.

- He is empowered by the law to inspect, investigate, recommend and to impose administrative penalties directly.

- Amongst the specific functions of the Ministry of supervision includes:

  - Supervision and inspection and implementation of those who supervise state policies, laws, decrees, national economic and social development plans as well as the decisions and orders promulgated by State Council.

  - To handle and investigate cases of violation of state laws, decrees, and breach of administrative disciplines and meet out disciplinary punishments.

- To study and examine the policies or regulations made by all the Departments under the State Council and the Local government and put forward recommendations for revision or amendments accordingly.

- Specific Supervisory organs in Governments from Provincial down to the country level have been established. Ministry of supervision comprises of 23 offices and Departments with a 1000 odd staff. Ministry has set up 50 branch offices in other ministries and Commissions under the State Council.

The other unique feature peculiar to the minister of supervision in China is that he examines and decides upon state laws and policies. In all the other countries the Ombudsman do not sit over the legislation they don not decide what legislation is good or bad. Legislations passed by the legislature are accepted as such by the Ombudsman in other countries. Similarly Ombudsman in countries does not examine or adjudicate upon the state policies. All state policies in other countries are decided by the political leaders, and assemblies, which enact the laws. In China Minister of Supervision is authorized to examine whether the law passed by the legislature is good for the nation and for the people.

ii. HONG KONG

The Hong Kong Ombudsman is officially known as the Commissioner for administrative complaints (COMAC). The Governor of Hong Kong appointed the first COMAC in 1989 under the COMAC Ordinance. The COMAC is an independent person outside the Public Service who reports directly to the Governor. Before 1994 COMAC could only investigate complaints referred to it by the Legislative Council Amendments to the COMAC Ordinance in MID-1994 brought some fundamental changes to the system, the more significant of which are the provisions to the need for referral and for COMAC to take a more proactive approach in addressing problems of potentially wide public interest and concern by undertaking direct investigation out of its own volition notwithstanding that no complaint has been lodged.

(a) SALIENT FEATURES

The salient features of COMAC (Hong Kong Ombudsman) are enumerated as under: -

I. Addresses issues arising from mal-administration in the public sector through independent, objective and impartial investigations.

II. COMAC many exercise his discretion to determine whether to undertake or discontinue with an investigation as well as decide the manner in which it is to be conducted.

III. COMAC may direct an investigation into the matter if he is of the opinion that any person may have sustained injustice as a consequence of mal-administration.

IV. COMAC has the power to call for information or documents from any person, summon witnesses and examine under oath, if necessary; enter, inspect and conduct investigation in any premises managed, occupied, or controlled by the concerned organization under his jurisdiction.

V. Enjoys jurisdiction on all Government Departments (61Govt. Departments and 14 statutory organizations).

(b) JURISDICTION OUSTED

The jurisdiction is ousted in respect of:

I. The Royal Hong Kong Police Force.

II. The Independent Commissioner against corruption (ICAC).

III. Major statutory organizations such as the Hong Kong Housing Authority, Hospital Authority, Mass Transit. Railway Corporation, important Municipal Councils etc.

ADMINISTRATIVE SETUP

The administrative setup comprises of:

(a) Investigation Division headed by Deputy Commissioner.

(b) A screening Division headed by Assistant Commissioner- it is complaint Registration Cell.

(c) Administrative Division headed by Principal executive officer.

(d) Staff of COMAC comprises of contract officers recruited directly, Civil servants mainly belonging to the Executive Grade seconded from the Government.

(e) COMAC does not prossess the executive powers to authoritatively require departments or organizations to implement its recommendations. He may, if circumstances warrant, bring the matter to the attention of the Governor, or through him to the Legislative Council.

(f) Conducting direct investigations of problems, which involved alleged or suspected maladministration and considerable public interest.

ACCESSIBILITY TO THE GENERAL PUBLIC.

Due emphasis has been laid to make COMAC system more accessible to the general public. To acquaint as the departments and public Organizations more about the COMAC system, following initiatives has taken: -

I. Touring and wide publicity whereby COMAC staff meets and receives complaints at the District Offices.

II. Enlisting of support of Non-Official justices of the Peace in referring complaints and bringing COMAC's attention to areas of public concerns or deficiencies of public administration.

III. Visiting of all departments and organizations under COMAC's jurisdiction with a view to promote mutual understandings.

IV. Production of an Administrative fairness checklist for the reference of departments and public Organizations within COMAC's jurisdiction.

V. Giving of talks to Universities, Institutes and Secondary Schools.

VI. Organization of workshops and seminars on complaint handling.

VII. Monitoring of meaningful youth involvement programs to install increased interest, commitment and support for the Ombudsman system.

PUBLIC AWARENESS ABOUT THE COMAC

Chapter XII

The COMAC has been established to serve the Hong Kong community. It is important that the public is made well aware of its existence and how it can help redress their grievances and improve the administration. COMAC has taken a number of initiatives to enhance public awareness and promote the system including the following:-

I. Production of a publicity Video on the COMAC system.

II. Release of announcements of Public Interest (APIs) and community service programmers to publicize COMAC's services on television and radio.

III. Mounting of Posters at prominent places frequented by members of the public.

IV. Staging of mobile exhibitions at6 major shopping arcad3s, Mass Transit Railway Stations and public housing estates.

V. Educating young people on the importance of fair, open , and efficient Government and nurturing a correct complaint culture by including the subject in the School curriculum for civic or public affairs education.

VI. Publishing anonymous investigation reports and complaint statistics in its monthly news letter 'COMAC NEWS'.

VII. Holding of Press Conferences to announce the results of direct investigations, the issue of COMAC News or other special events.

iii. INDIA

In India the nomenclature of LOKPAL/LOKAYUKTA is used for the institution of Ombudsman. Though efforts to establish this institution in India stated in 1960, yet it took concrete shape when on April 9, 1965, a resolution on the subject was moved in Parliament and a Special Consultative group of Members of Parliament on Administrative Reforms was constituted. This administrative Reforms Committee (ARC) recommended, through a bill, the establishment of a two tier machinery of LOKPAL and LOKAYUKTA, the former to deal with complaints against the Ministers and Secretaries to the Government at the Centre as well as in the States, and the latter (LOKAYUKTA) in each state and one at the Centre to deal with complaints against officials.

However, the scheme took another twenty years to make some progress and it was in August 1985 that Lok Sabah (Indian Parliament) considered the bill and handed it over to the Select Committee of the Parliament for consideration. Despite the urgency of the need, the institution of Lokpal could not be set up at the Central level till now. However certain state took the lead and Loakyuktas (Provincial Ombudsman) were established in Maharastra, Rajisthan, Uttar pardesh, Andra Pardesh and Hamachal Pardesh etc. Thus in all, nine states had passed the Lokayukta Acts during the period from 1978-1985. The Lokayukta Acts passed in various states are more less on the same pattern as that of the Lokayukta at the centre.

SALIENT FEATURES

I. The Governor of State appoints Lokayukta after consultation with the Chief Justice of the High Court and leader of the Opposition in the Assembly.

II. A person who has been the judge of the Supreme Court of India or Chief Justice of a High Court in India is qualified for appointment as Lokayukta (Ombudsman).

III. His terms of office are five years.

IV. Like Pakistan, the Ombudsman is not eligible for reappointment for the second term nor can be given extensions or further employment.

V. The procedure for removals similar to that of a judge of a Supreme Court and can be affected only on grounds of proved misconduct or incapacity.

VI. His salary is the same as admissible to a serving Judge of a High Court/ Supreme Court.

VII. He can utilize the services of (I) any officer or investigative Agency of the State or of the Central Government with concurrence of that Government and (ii) any other person or Agency.

VIII. Lokayukta is primarily concerned with corrective function and not punitive function.

iv. IRAN

"Being aware of a necessitating consistent organization for supervising and inspecting the proper conduct of executive affairs, a public organization of capable and confident people was organized. They were called the eyes and ears of the state. Their reports led to the redressed of grievances and punishment of those who violated rules and regulations.

Before the Islamic Resolution there existed in Iran two organizations for inspecting and controlling the public affairs one for Courts and the other for administrative organization. After the glorious Islamic Revolution, supervision of the whole administrative system of the country was specially provided in law as exponent in the principle No.174 of the constitutional law of the Islamic Republic of Iran reading as follows: -

> "On the basis of the right of supervision by the judiciary

> on the good conduct of affairs and proper implementation of laws by the administrative departments, an organization known as the 'State Chief Inspectorate' shall be established under the supervision of the Head of the Judiciary".

In pursuance of the above principle, the due rules for constituting the General Inspectorate organization of the Islamic Republic of Iran were passed and ratified in 1982 by the Islamic Consultative Assembly, Since then through the activities of the experienced Judges and efficient experts the organization has been exerting its duties, and had been removing the administrative executive and judicial inconveniences. As a result, it has been known as an active organization of high significance and dignity.

JURISDICTON

I. Constant controlling and supervising all the Ministries administration, Military Forces, Police, State run institutions and Companies, municipalities and offices associate with them, public notary departments, the institutions whose financial resources totally or partially belong to the Government and etc.

II. Extra Ordinary inspection would be implemented upon the order of the Head of the Judiciary, or required by the Commission of the Article 90 of the constitution of the Islamic Consultative Assembly, or Requested by a Minister or by the highest rank official of any executive organ or also any other instances which the head of the Inspectorate Organization discerns as necessary to be inspected.

III. Hearing the complainants and investigating the notifications. Real and Legal persons can notify their complaints against the organizations and institutions covered under the section above, to the General Inspectorate Organization. The notification and complaints may be relating to the Governmental sanctioned orders, regulations, circulars, orders by executive officials or the contingent violated private rights of the complainants.

To implement it's assigned duties, the Inspectorate Organization resort to following activities:-

I. Examining the institutions and organs in respect of proper conducting of affairs and duties, correct implementation of law, plans and programmers and considering the range of the development of each of those organs in proportion to the common requirements.

II. Investigating the behavior of the head the organization and that of the relating staff in respect of ethics, faith, morale, knowledge, equality of their proceeds, accuracy, capability and courage, their behaviour in confronting with the people referring to those organizations, the extent to their information and specialty in respect of their duties.

III. Investigating the common and social circumstances in respect to the common morale, economic affairs, agricultural and industrial productions, culture, hygiene, communications, roads judicial affairs, and common needs of the areas being inspected.

IV. On inspection, the General Inspectorate Organization would offer necessary suggestions for removing the inconveniences considered and also prosecute, through legal authorities those who have violated the law; and regulations. In case that it is proved that the orders, regulations and circulars are not consistent with the orders, regulations and circulars are not consistent with the rules made and ratified by the Islamic Consultative Assembly, a copy of the report would be sent to the Court of administrative justice for prompt proceedings.

In short, as the above details manifestly show that the jurisdictions of the General Inspection Organization are very extensive and very comprehensive as well".

v. IRAQ

Since recently Iraq has adopted dual judicial system namely "Ordinary Judicial System" and "Administrative

Judicial System". The Administrative judicial system is concerned with the redresses of complaints of the citizens and hence may called as "Institution of Ombudsman". Its jurisdiction and scope covers the control and check on the decision, decrees and orders issued by the Government Officials, functionaries and departments towards and against the citizens. The administrative judiciary which is not authorized to interfere in the affairs of the sovereignty, can competently look into and investigate:

I. To examine and determine whether the grievances or complaints by the citizens are valid or not.

II. To abrogate the decisions and decrees of the Government functionaries and officials against the citizens, if found justified.

III. To amend the decisions or orders against the interests of common people and,

IV. To issue orders for proper compensation to public resulting in the abrogation of unjustified decisions if so required by the plaintiff.

JURISDICTION

The Court of Administrative judiciary functions under the supervision of the General Authority of the Consultative Assembly of the State and has the jurisdiction of Supreme Court. The General Authority consists its president, two Vice Presidents, and a minimum number of twelve advisors. They render judgments with majority vote. The Advisors are appointed from amongst the judges of First Class, director Generals of the Ministry of Law and Justice, the attorney generals, and professors of law colleges".

vi. JAPAN

Chapter XII

"Administrative Inspection Bureau (AIB) of the Management and Coordination Agency (MCA) is the equivalent of Ombudsman institutions in other countries of Asia. It is an independent organization of the Prime Minister's Office and is headed by a Minister of State (member of Cabinet). Its functions are administrative inspection and administrative counseling and are carried out by 1,200 staff. They together provide an effective system of administrative supervision and relief, ensuring that public administration is conducted in a democratic, effective, efficient, and fair manner, protecting the rights and interests of the citizens, and thereby securing the trust of 120 million people of Japan in their government.

Japan has a parliamentary system of government. The government is held accountable to the public through the Diet. The Courts and the independent Board of Audit are other system to ensure administrative accountability.

The administrative inspection and the administrative counseling are the functions within the executive branch of the government to hold the administrative organs accountable to the public.

The Management and Coordination Agency Establishment Law provide that one of its functions is "to inspect the operation of administrative organ, and make recommendations if deemed necessary".

For the purpose of performing the function, the (Art, 4,CI.12).gives Director General of the MCA necessary authority including those of (1) demanding the head of administrative organs submission of materials and explanations (Art, 5, Para 2) and (ii) making on-site investigation of the operation of administrative organs (Art.5, Para). The authority is internally delegated to the heads of AIB field offices.

Chapter XII

The objective of administrative inspection by MCB is to maintain the effectiveness of government, to prevent unlawful or improper practice and damages to the national treasury, and to maintain official discipline.

Based on the analysis and evaluation of the facts found and evidence collected by the 600 of the AIB headquarters and field offices, the Director General of MCA makes recommendations for improvement to other ministers. The ministers concerned are required to report to the MCA Director General on the measures taken pursuant to the recommendations. The Director General may also report to the Prime Minister his opinion requesting that a direction be issued to the ministers concerned to improve matters under their jurisdictions.

It has contributed to elimination of mis-use of funds and other corrupt practices, introduction and reform of police and procedures, and improvement of government, all in keeping with the demands of the times.

The administrative counseling was started around 1955. in 1961, system of administrative counselors was introduced also as an operational arrangement for the purpose of broadening the system's base and enhancing the accessibility to the people of administrative counseling service. In 1966, the Administrative Counselors a solid statutory base. The system dramatically improved the people's access to the administrative counseling system both in geographic and psychological terms.

The Administrative Counseling is an activity in which the AIB file offices and the administrative counselors throughout the country receive citizen's complaints about he actions of the government agencies and act to bring the matters to a satisfactory conclusion through mediation.

The Administrative Counselors Law provides that the Director General of the MCA may commission " a person who enjoys a social confidence and is possessed of a deep understanding and ardor for improvement in administrative operation" for the work of (I) receiving peoples complaints, giving necessary advices and informing the MCA (AIB field offices) and the administrative organs concerned (Art.2,Para. 1) Today they are over 5,000 of them and people can find at least one of them and people can find at least one of them in the area of municipalities they live in. In many cases, satisfactory solutions are obtained by simply forwarding the complaints to the agencies concerned. Many cases are actually resolved by the administrative counselors studying the background and getting in touch with the government agencies concerned and the latter reviewing the case.

Complaints can be filed free of change either by phone, by letter, or by visits. There is no restriction on the subject of complaints except that cases falling into a number of categories including those pending in courts will not be eligible for mediation.

In the national government, the ministries and agencies operate counseling units of their own.

The work of most Ombudsman institutions in other countries appears to entail the elements of administrative supervision and administrative relief. As it happened, the AIB in Japan came to embody these very elements in its work as a consequence of unique historic development that gave it the functions of administrative inspection and administrative counseling independent of the development of Ombudsman institution another parts of the world.

There is also an advisory body to the Director General called the Administrative Grievance Resolution Promotion Council. It is composed of seven private individuals from the judicial circle, mass media and others. It maximizes fairness and impartiality in AIB's operation of administrative counseling and make it as close as possible in practice to that of submitted to the Director General a large number of opinions which were reflected in mediations to result in important changes in the system and practice of administration that benefited not only the complainants but also other members of the Public".

vii. JORDAN

Realizing the importance the importance of establishing organization to fight corruption and to monitor the performance of public institutions, the Bureau of Administrative Inspection and Control came into existence in 1992. It performs administrative control over the ministries and departments of the

Jordanian Government. The Bureau factually acts as an Ombudsman like institution for the redressal of grievances of ordinary citizens against public authorities.

viii. KOREA

The Ombudsman of Korea was established in April,1994 by the Basic Act on Administrative Regulations and Civil complaints which upholds the fairness and transparency of public administration and protects citizen's rights. The Presidential decree of 1949 provided common procedures and standards for all administrative Agencies. In 1971, the offices of the Joint Government Counseling Service (JGCS) were created to take whole responsibility for receiving and resolving a wide range of complaints and grievances against public administration. The improvements so for achieved in simplifying the administrative procedure, have yet to achieve success. But for reluctance and resistance of the Ministries concerned with any bureaucratic powers and the possible adverse effects as a results of deregulation, there still remained a number of problems a complexity of laws and regulations, discrepancies between unrealistic rules and practices, a vicious circle of the relaxation of existing regulations and new regulation or deregulations, confusion surrounding ambiguous criteria and discretionary interpretations, irksome administrative processes and excessive paper work requirements.

On the other hand, the JGCS scheme was not used as much as originally expected, it was probably due to weakness of a legal basis for its functions and powers. Major portions of complaints received by the JGCS could not be investigated and handled by its own staffs, and were merely transferred to the agencies concerned. The result was that the services were not able to come up to the Ordinary people's expectations, whereas the public was tolerant of any breach of courtesy, delay and laxity in the government's administration.

Now the Basic Act mentioned above led to establish the Ombudsman of Korea in order to maximize the capacity of complaints handling and to secure the public's trust in Government. Though the ministries and other organization also resolve the citizen's grievances yet the JGCS has occupied the Central position in the overall structure of complaints resolution mechanism. However most of the Agencies and Local Governments are naturally reluctant to admit and correct their own mistakes and usually make plausible excuses. This is simply because public officials tend to adhere strictly to precedents and texts providing laws and guidelines. The JGCS (Joint Government Counseling Service) which was created in 1971 are re-organized in 1980 to undertake a number of functions as follows".

I. To receive and process grievances concerning the operation of the Government, and provide necessary information and consulting service;

II. To guide and inspect the counseling units of each administrative agencies including local authorities, for the purpose of ensuring their civil applications for permits and licenses, etc. are administered in a fair, expeditious and democratic manner;

III. To operate the system of administrative Counselors in local authorities.

The J.G.C.S, however, can not handle following (Bar of Jurisdiction)

I. A case, which required political or highly technical consideration;

II. A case under criminal investigation;

III. A case pending in administrative litigation of administrative appeal / review procedures by the competent administrative bodies;

IV. Decision of the Court has been issued as a result of the procedure cited in the above 3 cases.

THE OMBUDSMAN OF KOREA

16.39 The Ombudsman of Korea was established in April 1994 upon the enactment of the Basic Act on Administrative Regulations and Civil complaints. The Ombudsman has the legal power to investigate complaints and to make and publicize its subpoena recommendation. It also has the power to subpoena witnesses, to investigate documents and to her evidences, and to assess the information held by any Government Agency.

The Ombudsman is able to address administrative actions that are;

I. Contrary to laws or regulations'

II. Unreasonable, unfair, oppressive, or inconsistent with the general course of an administrative Agency's functions'

III. Mistaken in laws or arbitrary in ascertainment of facts;

IV. Improper in motivation or based on irrelevant consideration;

V. Unclear or inadequately explained when reasons should have been revealed.

VI. Inefficiently performed, or

VII. Otherwise objectionable.

After reviewing a complaint, the Ombudsman can state the recommendation (s) to the agency concerned if the Ombudsman has the opinion that an administrative Agency should consider the matter further, modify/cancel administrative actions, provide a more comprehensive explanations of the actions in question, or take any other step after regulations, or procedures to prevent similar complaint, or take any other steps. The agency, if so requested should inform the Ombudsman of the actions taken on the recommendations or the reasons for not complying with them within 30 days. The Ombudsman should submit an annual report on the operation of the Ombudsman to the President and publish it to the public.

The basic act gives the Ombudsman the power to investigate only the received complaints. The term 'administrative agency', means any department, office or office or other unit of both central and local governments of any public Corporation, association or individual who exercises the entrusted administrative authority, but the 'Administrative agency does not include the President, Courts or judges, members of the National Assembly. The BAL (The Board of Audit and Inspection) and Local Councils.

An 'Administration work' includes every action (such as decisions, omissions, in-action, recommendations practices or procedures) of an administrative agency.

JURISDICTION OUSTED

The Ombudsman does not have jurisdiction over the following

I. Relating to personal privacy;

II. Which fall under the prosecutorial jurisdiction;

III. For which administrative appeal and litigation procedures under other relevant laws are in progress;

IV. Cases for which settlement procedures between the parties are in progress by way of compromise, mediation,

V. Matters, which have been settled through the procedures of administrative appeal or compromise on conciliation.

VI. Matters, which have been settled through the procedures of administrative appeal or compromise on conciliation.

VII. Matter, which the Ombudsman considers in- appropriate to be handled. In fact in matters where he has reason to believe that the complainant's interest is trivial, frivolous, not made in good faith, or complaint is too old.

ORGANISATIONAL PATTERN

The Ombudsman of Korea is attached to the Prime Minister and the Government officers of the JGCS undertake the whole task of the Ombudsman. The Ombudsman of Korea is composed of 5 Ombudsmen, including one standing Ombudsman. The President of Korea appoints or Commissions the Chief Ombudsman and 4 other Ombudsman from amongst the civilians recommended by the social organization and one from the senior serving or retired Government servant.

The tenure of the Ombudsman is for 3 years and can be renewed once. To ensue the independent status of the Ombudsman of Korea, the Ombudsman can not be a member of the National Assembly, Local Councils, Political parties, and can not be an employee of Organization or Corporations having special relationship with administrative Agencies. The Ombudsman should not infringe on the jurisdiction of the Ministers as stated in the Basic Act.

The important feature of the Korean Ombudsman is seen in the fact that while some countries under the Parliamentary system have Parliamentary Ombudsman, the Korean Ombudsman is an administrative Ombudsman.

ix. MACAO

Chapter XII

Macao-a Chinese territory located on the Pearl River Delta at a distance of about 70 Kilometers from Hong Kong and 153 Kilometers form Canton, is known for its social and cultural pluralism and hence distinct from other countries. Under the terms of a 1987 agreement between Portugal and China, the administration of the territory had reverted to the People's Republic of China on 20th, December 1999. Macau now has the status of a special administrative region with independent legislative, executive and judicial powers. During the transition period covering about 50 years much had been done to strengthen the values, which single out and define Macao's identity.

The Macao Public Administration is committed to sobriety, honesty, transparency, competence, and respect for the legally protected rights and interests of its citizens. It is in this context that the High Commission against corruption and administrative illegality was created in July 1990 to protect the rights and legitimate interests of Macau's inhabitants. The High commission is a public body independent, high authority within the administration. Its object is to receive complaints from private individuals concerning the behavior of public bodies. It uses its authority and powers of persuasion to lead public bodies to make reparations for any injustice or illegal act that they may have committed or to alter decision based on bad management that they may have taken.

The High commission was created after the model of the Ombudsman-an institution of Nordic Origin also known as 'Mediateur" in France, Portecteur des citoyens' in Quebgec, Difensore Civico' in some regions of Italy and 'Defensive del Pueblo' in Spain. All these terms reflect, according to the feelings of the various peoples the essence of its duties to promote the effective exercise of Citizen's legally protected rights, freedoms, safeguard, and interests._This is a universal model whose limitless essence is dominated by the ideas of justice and good, eternal human concerns. In the face of new challenges brought by a world in constant change, these institutions have been playing an increasingly relevant role regardless of geographical location or political regime, so long there is democracy.

In order to protect the legitimate rights, freedom, safeguards, and interests of Macau's people, the High Commission has a broad range of powers permitting it to:

- Access the legality and justice of administrative acts or procedures concerning private individuals;
- Supervise the lawfulness and administrative correctness of acts involving property interest;
- Denounce the relevant bodies for punitive actions and punish signs of breaches of which it becomes aware.
- Supervise the progress of any case dealt with by the relevant bodies with powers to deal with disciplinary or criminal proceedings.

- Propose to the Governor or the Legislative Assembly that legislative measures are taken to improve the operations of public departments and enhance respect for administrative legality.

- Propose to the Governor that administrative measures be taken with a view to improve public services.

- Cooperate with the relevant bodies and public departments of find the most suitable solutions for protecting people's legislative interests and to enhance administrative actions.

- To publicize, in the media its acts in pursuing the goals.

Access to the High Commission is guaranteed to ever body, either individually or in a group and also or private collective persons. Any private individual may take a complaint about any illegal or unfair act or about in the running of any department. The high commission may also, on its initiative, open an investigation of facts of which it has learned in any way. Public bodies should also inform the High Commissioner of any criminal or disciplinary of infraction of which they have knowledge, and of the final decisions, of any cases.

Complaints or denunciation should be submitted personally and directly to the High Commission in written documents, which do not have to conform to any special form or specific proceedings. The document is addressed to the High Commissioner and submitted to the High Commission by post, telegraph, telex, fax, or any other means of communication. There is also a 24 hours hot line.

In order to provide due to the restraint complaint, the high Commission after through investigation and enquiry may order as under or take any of the listed measures.

- Recommend to the relevant authorities that it make reparations for the illegal or unjust act, by modifying, canceling or revoking its actions.
- Recommend to the relevant administrative authorities criteria for the correct interpretations of legal norms.
- Propose the evaluation of, whether norms are unconstitutional or illegal.
- Point out to the relevant organs any legislation that is missing or insufficient.
- Suggest the adoption of administrative measures, which could simplify administrative procedures and bureaucratic circuits;
- Clarify the persons making the complaints, or to the public in general, any act concerning the management of public affairs brought to the light by the complaint or about which there is any doubt.
- Inform the person making complaint of the method or approach he should

adopt in order to have a right recognized, and interest protected, or damaged made good.

- Use the media as a final method for responding to the public opinion, both for providing information about the unresolved situation of injustice and for publicizing letters reports or official memoranda concerning cases in which no reparation has been made for an offence committed.

From the above discussion it had been seen that the High commissioner has no decision making power. He can not order, decide, or impose. However, he can make recommendations, suggestions, criticism, and comments. He can also encourage, inspect or spread information. Through his independence, he can play informal control of acts practiced by the administrative organs, as a mediator in conflicts between these and citizens, as a mediator as a provider of reforms aimed at safeguarding legality, transparency, and injustice.

His power and legitimacy derives from his ability to carry out efficient and publicly recognized actions aimed at creating better conditions for quality, quick and fair behavior on the part of the administration and at making relationship between the administration and Macau' citizens closer and more humane.

x. MALAYSIA

In Malaysia, managing of the public complaints us being handled by the Public complaints bureau on the Prime minister's department. P.C.B. was established in July 1971 with the main objective of to assist the who are aggrieved with the public service machinery and to take remedial actions towards redressing complaints that are justified and to utilize complaints in an input for Government agencies to improve accountability, quality, and productivity in the Public service.

P.C.B. derives its power from Development Administration circular No.4 of 1992. P.C.B. is designed as the center for public complaints with responsibilities and functions as follows:-

a):- To receive public complaints on government administrative actions which are alleged to be unfair, agents the existing laws and regulations including misconduct, misappropriation, abuse of power, maladministration and the like.

b):- To investigate public complaints which are deemed to be valid.

c):- To report the outcome of investigation and make recommendation to the permanent committee on public complaints (PCPC) and authorities.

d):- To forward the decision of PCPC to Ministers, Federal

Departments, Federal statutory Bodies, Local authorities, Agencies concerned for the purpose of the corrective actions.

e):- To monitor the actions taken by the ministries, federal departments, federal statutory bodies, local authorities, agencies concerned and subsequently submit such feedback to the PCPC.

PERMANENT COMMITTEE ON PUBLIC COMPLAINTS

16.59 PCPC is chaired the Chief Secretary to the Government and members of the Committee are:-

I The Director General of the Public services Department.

II The Director General of the Anti corruption Committee.

III The Senior Deputy Secretary General of the Prime Minister's Department.

Chapter XII

TERMS OF REFERNCE.

- To formulate policies on the system of managing Public complaints.
- To consider and make decisions on reports cases submitted by the Public complaint bureau on public complaints.
- To direct Secretary General of ministries, head of statutory authorities, head of local authorities, head of agencies, concerned to attend meetings of PCPC to explain specific cases/complaints.
- To direct Ministries/Federal Departments/Local authorities/ Agencies concerned to take remedial actions to resolve complaints refer to them.

The Membership of these head of agencies in PCPC is to ensure that all Government agencies provide full co-operation to the system of management of public complaints and to resolve all complaints effectively and speedily. Every year PCB handles thousands of complaints pertaining to delays in carrying the official duties, unfair decisions or actions, lack of public services or utilities inadequate or bias rules and procedures, abuses of power, misconducts of public servants, inefficiencies of public servants and failure to enforce regulations and laws based upon the cases investigated by PCB, the recommended disciplinary actions against the several government servants who had been negligent or had abused their powers while carrying out their duties.

xi. MALDIVES

There is no such permanent institute in Maldives but to some extent there exist arrangement to redress the people's grievances. Maldives comprises of over 1000 islands but only 202 are inhabited divided into 19 provinces. Each province has a chief who acts as an incharge of the area. In each island an office has been established to which people lodge their complaints and their grievances redressed. This is in addition to regular courts.

Chapter XII

xii MANILA (FILLIPINES)

The ombudsman at Manila is characterized by extra-ordinary broad and comprehensive powers not usually available to other Asian Ombudsman to eliminate graft and corruption from the public offices. For prosecuting the erring government officials, he has the services of a special prosecutor (A senior police officer of the rank of the **DIG** in Pakistan). His office is an official independent constitutional body created by the constitution. The ombudsman, if warranted by evidence, can competently file and prosecute criminals, civil, or administrative cases before the relevant courts or administrative body. The objective is tom come up to expectations of the people as their protector in the real sense so as to promote efficient services by the government of Philippines is also known as the 'TANODBAYAN' which means protector of the people or "Sentinel of the Nation".

Chapter XII

Like other offices of the Ombudsmen of the world, the Ombudsmen of Philippine receives and investigates complaints receives and investigates complaints relating to all sorts of public offices whether government owned or controlled corporations and make appropriate recommendations having the force of a decision. In fact graft prevention office, which determine the causes of in-efficiency, red tape, mis-management, fraud and corruption in the government. The observance of high standards of ethics and efficiency of the government agencies constitute one of its main functions.

The Ombudsmen's Office at manila became operational on May 12, 1988 simultaneous to the appointment of Ombudsman at Manila and Deputy Ombudsman each for Luzen, Visayas, and Mindanae. However for effectively carrying out the mandate, the relevant Republic Act No.6770 (one wise known as the Ombudsmen Act of 1989) delineating its powers, functions and duties came on ground on 17th November,1987.

The other distinctive characteristics of the Ombudsmen at Manila are: -

I. The Ombudsmen is appointed by the President from a list of six nominees prepared by the higher judiciary and bar Council for a term of seven years with no provision for extension or re-employment. The recognized probity, independence and professionalism are the requisite qualifications for his selection as an Ombudsman.

II. A criminal complaint may be brought for an

offence in violation of 'Anti-graft and corrupt Practices Act as amended R.A. 1379 (An act declaring forfeiture in favour of state any property found to have been unlawfully acquired by any public officer or employee as per R.A-6713 (Code of Conduct and Ethical Standards for public Officials and Employees).

III. The Resident Ombudsmen serves as the deputized Ombudsmen investigator. He is authorized to conduct, fact-finding enquiries in matters falling within his functions and for such purpose, shall be deemed empowered to issue subpoena and subpoena ducestecum.

IV. The Ombudsmen embarks on Community programmed aimed at institutionalizing a partnership between the government and the public sector in its crusade to minimize, if not completely eradicate graft and corruption in the public service. This includes setting up of the Corruption Prevention Units (CPUS) aimed to broaden community participation in the fight against corruption and red tape in the bureaucracy. The CPUS in NGOs(Non government organizations), student organizations, etc. are the Ombudsman's eyes and arms which will closely monitor critical and substantially funded government projects.

Apart from the usual functions of investigation into the intentional commission of offences such as abuses of law and acts of dishonesty (malfeasance) incompetence and incompetence and inefficiency (misfeasance) inaction and indifference (nonfeasance), the Ombudsman entertains complaints entertains complaints for such acts of omission of a public official alleged to be unreasonable, unfair, oppressive, discriminatory, improper or inefficient though it may not necessarily amount to a criminal administrative offence.

In addition to the above the manifestations of maladministration, which call for the intervention of Ombudsman, are:

(a) If the alleged action is inconsistent with the general course of agency's functions though in accordance with law.

(b) On a mistake of law or an arbitrary ascertainment of factors.

(c) In the exercise of discretionary powers but for and improper purpose.

(d) Otherwise irregular and immoral or;

(e) Due to any delay or refusal to comply with the referral of directive of the Ombudsman or any of his deputies or employee to whom it was addressed; and,

(f) Such other grounds provided for under P.D.807 R.A.6713 and other applicable laws.

xiii. PAKISTAN

The extracts of the paper read by Mr. Justice (Rtd) Abdul Shakurual Salam, MOHTASIB (OMBUDSMAN) of PAKISTAN in First Asian Ombudsman Conference held in Islamabad on 15th-16th April, 1996, being authentic and elaborately well presented, are reproduced.

His paper provides details of the salient features, powers and working procedure of the Ombudsman in Pakistan in a most befitting manner,

STATUTORY PROVISIONS

The constitution of Pakistan provides for an Ombudsman on the Federal list who is appointed on the advice of the Prime Minister by the President. Having approval of both the Heads of the Government and the state, he discharges his duties without any fear and favour. He is removable only by judicial impeachment. The issue of appointing Provincial Ombudsman is left to the Provincial Legislature.

The office of Ombudsman was established under the Establishment of the Office of Wafaqi Mohtasib (Ombudsman) order 1983 (President's Order No.1 of 1983). Article 9 of the said order provides that Ombudsman may on a motion of the supreme Court or a High Court made during the course of any proceedings before it or of his own motion, undertake any Agency or any of its officers or employees, except when the matter is sub judice, relates to the external affairs of Pakistan or to the defense of Pakistan. Vide Article 2(2), maladministration includes: “(I) a decision, process, recommendation, act of mission or commission which: (a) is contrary to law, rules or regulations or is a departure from established practice or procedure, unless it is bonafide and for valid reasons ;or (b) is perverse, arbitrary or unreasonable, unjust, biased, oppressive, or discriminatory; or (c) is based on irrelevant grounds; or (d) involves the exercise of powers or the failure or refusal to do so, for corrupt or improper motives, such as , bribery, jobbery, favoritism , nepotism and administrative excesses; and (ii) neglect, inattention, delay, incompetence, inefficiency and ineptitude, in the administration or discharge of duties and responsibilities. “The Agency is defined under Article 2(1) to mean “ a Ministry, Division, Department, Commission or office of the Federal Government or statutory corporation or other institution established or controlled by the Federal Government but does not include the Supreme Court, The Supreme Judicial Council, the Federal shariat Court or a High Court." or a High Court." Under Article 3(3), the "independently of the executive" and "all executive authorities throughout Pakistan shall act in aid of the Mohtasib".

Recommendations of the Ombudsman are required to be implemented or reasons for non-compliance are to be given under Article 11(2). In case of defiance, the matter can be reported to the Preside4nt under Article 11(5) read with Article 12. The defaulting functionaries. The recalcitrant can also be punished under the provisions for contempt of court vide Article 16, Article 33 authorizes the Ombudsman notwithstanding anything in the Order, to informally conciliate, amicably resolve, settle or ameliorate any grievance without legal formalities. Under Article 29, "no court or other authority shall have jurisdiction (I) to question the validity of any action taken, or intended to be taken, or order made, or anything done or purporting to have been taken, made or done under this Order, or (ii) to grant an injection or stay or to make any interim order in relation to any proceeding before, or anything done or intended to be done or purporting to have been done by, or under the orders or at the instance of the Mohtasib". Under Article 32, any person aggrieved by a decision or order of Mohtasib, may within thirty days, make a representation to the President who may pass such order as he may deem fit. This right is for a person who has not been granted relief by the Mohtasib for any limitation of law or otherwise. The President may grant him relief in his discretion. However, this right of representation cannot be evoked by any Agency defined in Article 29 aforementioned to question any action taken or order made by the Mohtasib under the Order.

Chapter XII

PRESIDENT'S DIRECTIVE

On 20th September 1990, the President issued the directive that the Ombudsman's institution has been established to render inexpensive and speedy justice to the poor and downtrodden citizens, aggrieved or affected by the act of maladministration of the Federal Agencies. So, to ensure that relief is provided to the common man against the excesses and acts of maladministration of the Federal Government Functionaries, Recommendation/Findings of the Wafaqi Mohtasib (Ombudsman) should be implemented within the stipulated time. All Federal Agencies were urged to extend full co-operation to the Ombudsman for carrying out his functions smoothly in accordance with the requirements of law.

PRIME MINISTER'S DIRECTIVE

On 14th November 1995, the prime Minister of Pakistan directed all Federal Agencies to strictly follow, both in letter and spirit, the directions of the President, and in future compliance should be made promptly in respect of the cases involving pensions, gratuities, or other benefits arising on the retirement; for giving preference in the employment to widow or children of deceased / retired employees in grade 1 to 11 as per recruitment rules; for appointment of women against their reserved quotas; medical expenses; insurance claims; utilities bills; compensation or remuneration allowed to the widows, orphans, invalids or incapacitated, persons where the amount is not more than the Rs.5 million in an individual case and is permissible under the law.

ORGAINIZATION AND THE SYSTEM

The Ombudsman, has its Headquarters Office at Islamabad and also Regional Offices in the capital of the four Provinces of Pakistan i.e. Punjab at Lahore, Sindh at Karachi, NWFP at Peshawar and Baluchistan at Quetta. These Offices have been manned by; selection of officers from the Government, retired judges of the High courts or senior retired public servants who had the aptitude and experience to redress the grievances of people. At the moment they are 50 in number.

A person aggrieved needs only send an application in any language pointing out his grievances. It is examined by the Registrar and Director General. If it has no substances at all or totally with out jurisdiction, it is proposed to reject for final order of an officer. Otherwise, it is sent to the Investigating Officer to probe the facts, call for report from the Agency concerned, hear the parties if necessary and recommend relief as far as permissible under the law. The findings and Recommendations are put up to the Ombudsman. On his approval and under his signature, these are then issued.

The findings and recommendations of the Ombudsman are invariably implemented and seldom delayed beyond the prescribed time. Most of the time all the authorities and others carry out the recommendations quite promptly. Even in matters where the jurisdiction of Ombudsman does not extend, like the Provincial field and local bodies etc., when the matter is taken up informally for settlement under Article 33 of P.O.I. of 1981, the authorities co-operate, send report, and care lot the recommendations.

EFFICACY

The job has been done with dedication and diligence and innumerable people have been granted relief. It is for this reason that more and more people approached the Ombudsman for solution of their problems. Even when no relief can be granted, the aggrieved person is, at least, explained the position and is so solaced. This is no mean a service.

It is common knowledge that people suffer in silence and can hardly bear their burden. Some of it is on account of poverty, illiteracy or ignorance. But their life can be a lot lightened, if the people who rule over them can envisage their problems, feel the miseries, and try to do what they can. Even if they were to listen to their woes, much can be done with a will. Inaccessibility and apathy led the people to lose confidence. The modern states' field of operation is so vast that the moment a child is born, he/ she has born, he /she is required to be registered with a public authority, for what is called birth certificate. When a person dies, the fact is to be reported by the bereaved again, to an authority. All his or her life, he/she is never free of the control and dependence on the State. Its officials after few years of the feel of authority become remote and insensitive. When approached for resolution of a problem, the first reaction is that relief is not possible because of this rule or that. If a moment were to be spared to' think' what can be done, the law or the rule would guide to the solution to the solution because these were for the benefit of the people, not to thwart their expectations and aspirations.

Against this background, Ombudsman's Organization is a boon for poor people. It investigates his complaint and helps in redressing his grievances. Even though it may be a drop in the ocean and its activities not dramatic, yet bit-by-bit it can encompass a vast area. No body is unaware that the problems are many and of colossal magnitude. More efforts are needed.

The moment ordinary grievances of the people arising in day to day living are resolved / redressed; efforts would be made for making suggestions to improve the functioning of the Government institutions so that those dealing with the people act quickly, efficiently and honestly in accordance with law, equity and good conscience.

xiv. SRILANKA

Accountability of Public Service and of Government institutions in SriLanka is ensured in diverse ways and means. There is Parliament and at question time Minister have to answer and account for the policies and practices pursued by Department,

Statutory Authorities and other state Bodies that come under their ministerial purview. Besides the regular courts, there is also a Public Service Commission with whom Public officials lodge complaints relating to grievances arising from the appointments, promotions, transfers, dismissals and such similar actions. A Chairman and cosnsisits of other members from experienced and eminent citizens head commission. It is an independent body and its impartiality is adequately safeguarded.

THE PARLIAMENTARY COMMISSIONER FOR ADMINISTRATION

The Parliamentary Commissioner for administration was provided for in Article 156 (Chapter XIX) of the Constitution of the Democratic Socialist Republic of Sri Lanka in 1978. He was charged with the duty of investigating and reporting upon complaints or allegations of the infringement of fundamental rights and other injustices by public Officers and Officers of Public Corporation, Local bodies, and other institutions in accordance with and subject to the provisions of law. As an appointee of the President, his tenure of office and terms and conditions of Office are secure so long his conduct and behavior are unimpeachable. The Article gives him wide powers and rights to discharge his duties independently without fear or favour.

In terms of the above constitutional provision, a further piece of legislation, Parliamentary Commissioner for Administration Act No. 17 of 1981, was enacted and a Parliamentary Commissioner was first appointed in 1982. The Act was amended in 1994 to make the institution more viable as since from the very beginning the Parliamentary Commissioner is commonly and popularly known as Ombudsman of Sri Lanka. The amended law has risen his retiring age to 70 years.

Before the amendment of 1994 petition had to be lodged through a Member of Parliament, and from 1st Februarys 1995 Petition could be directly addressed to the

Parliamentary commissioner for Administration. Direct access made conditions easier and less cumbersome. The procedure of investigation is not much different as practiced by the Ombudsman Act in Pakistan. In regard to the relief or the redress, be it in the form of restoration to a job after unjust dismissal or the grant of a due promotion that was withheld or an appointment to a position that was unreasonably not granted, the decision taken is communicated to the appropriate quarters with a copy of it to the Minister concerned and another coy to the Public Petitions Committee of Parliament. The parliamentary Commissioner for the execution of his determination allows reasonable period of time. If it is not executed then he should be provided with a report stating the reasons for non-compliance. The Parliamentary Commissioner for Administration forwards the report of the Agency along with a copy of his decision with his further comments to the President and to the Parliament both for any further action. This may take the form of further enquiry, if necessary, by the President, or could be a question in Parliament. But very few officials would relish this consequence and very often determinations (decisions) are complied with.

Generally the Parliamentary Commissioner for Administration endeavours to get both parties to an enquiry, the complainant and the alleged wrong doer, to agree on a settlement once allegations reasonably proven. There is an earnest attempt to mediate and conciliate this leaves the two parties to go out with less heart burning or a hostile and antagonistic attitude.

Where systems are wanting, the deficiencies are indicated and advice is rendered to supply them. Similarly, whenever rules, regulations and practices are unfair, corrections are commanded. The objective is to prevent repetition of wrongdoing and errors and to make public management turn out to be more effective, efficient and human.

Chapter XII

The law of parliamentary Commissioner for Administration in SriLanka has a unique provision and power distinct from other Ombudsman system of other Countries. It empowers the Parliamentary Commissioner to call for probe into evidence or to question witness's material to any inquiry into complaint. Non co-operation of any official in such an exercise can be reported through a certificate to a High court and the officials are tried. If found to be culpable, the official is liable to either a stipulated period of imprisonment or a defined money as a fine or both penalties together could be imposed. The security of tenure has ensured freedom from Ministerial interference.

The most common and usual grievances are;

- Non-payment of compensation or sufficient amount for acquisition of lands and buildings for urgent public purposes.

- The delay in making payments those are due.
- Unfair acquisitions of lands and Buildings.
- Discrimination in the allocation of public housing.
- Failure to allocate houses where applications deserve to receive them.
- Denial of equality in treatment by a public authority or discrimination in treatment in respect of appointment or promotion in statutory bodies.
- Denial of equality in treatment by a public authority or discrimination in treatment in respect of appointment or promotion in statutory bodies.
- Delays in payment of pensions and gratuity or wrong calculations of the amounts due.

- Dismissals from Corporations or similar public bodies if alleged to be unfair, not in accordance with rules or procedure or it are complained that the right to be heard in defence had been denied.

After due enquiry and investigation, Parliamentary Commissioner may recommend the matter to be reconsidered, an omission be rectified and the decision be cancelled or varied.

JURISDICTION OUSTED

No enquiry can be instituted in respect of:

- Powers, duties, or functions discharged in terms of the Legislation governing public security.

- Any decision or action of the Attorney General, Solicitor, General, or Departmental Legal Officer.

- Into the terms of services of security forces or any order given to a Security Officer by a Superior.
- Into any matter that is or has been before the Court.
- Appointments etc. of public Officers.
- Any decision of the Auditor General, Commissioner of Elections or an earlier Ombudsman or Parliamentary Commissioner.

The Parliamentary Commissioner is required to submit an Annual Report in addition to the reports sent at the end of each inquiry to the Public petitions Committee to the president of the Republic and to Parliament. This ensures his answerability and restrains him from resorting to unaccountable behaviour.

To sum up, the institution of the Parliamentary Commissioner for

Administration provides to the citizen an easy; economical and expeditious means to gain equity. As an institution it also acts as a deterrent to maladministration in public administration and as a spur to efficient management. He provides vigilance over public administration and thereby enhances good governance.

CHAPTER 13

INERTNATIONAL PICTURE OF OMBUDSMAN'S ORGANIZATION ABROAD

Chapter XIII

Chapter XIII

INERTNATIONAL PICTURE OF OMBUDSMAN'S ORGANIZATION ABROAD

At present, there are 270 Ombudsman institution in 114 countries of the world out of these tow major institution at International level representing the Ombudsman of various countries/region are the international Ombudsman institute (lOl) and the Asian Ombudsman association (AOA). Pakistan is a member of the board of Directors of the International Ombudsman institute (lOl) since 1984, President of the Asian Ombudsman Association (AOA), since its initiation in 1996 and has been taking active part in the regular meetings held by the two organizations.

International Ombudsman institute (IOI)

The Ombudsman institute (IOI) is a non-government organization, wich was established in1978, with is head quarter based at the university of Alberta

Edmonton Canada, it was incorporated as a none profit organization under the Canada Corporation Act. Its objective inter alia include support of the concept of the Ombudsman ship and to encourage its development throughout the world,to in encourage and support research to develop and operate educational Programmers associated with Ombudsman ship and to collects, store and giving out information about he Ombudsman institute (Article-5 of bye-laws).

As present the total voting membership of IOI is 163. IOI governed by the Board of Directors, which presently consists of 20 members represent different regions of the world. For carrying out the business of the instate board of Directors has ratified bye that laws in November 2000.The Board of Directors meets every years and the General meeting in the shape of a conference is regularly held every fourth years the membership of the International Ombudsman institute is not restricted to the Ombudsman institute is not restricted to the ombudsman institute an in entire at country. Any smaller organization which functions as an ombudsman, either at country level or at provincial / district level or even in a private capacity, can become a member of the IOI. Members of the IOI have been classified in to institutional members, associate members, individual Members, honorary life Members and Library Members.

The Wifaqi Mohtasib (Ombudsman)'s institution became Members of the Ombudsman institute (IOI) in the April 1984, right after its establishment and has continuously maintained its membership of the international Ombudsman institute from the Asian region. Being the largest institution in terms of handling the bulk of complaints, Pakistan was first time elected a member of the board of directors in 1993. Since then it has maintained its position as Director. Subsequently the Federal Tax Ombudsman, Provincial Ombudsman Punjab, and Ombudsman of Azad Jammu & Kashmir also became the Voting Members of the IOI .The last general meeting/Conference of International Ombudsman institute IOI was held November 2000 in Durban, South Africa. Whereas, the last meeting of the Board of Directors was held in Quebec City, Canada on 3rd October 2003.

Update On Asian Ombudsman Association (AOA)

Asian Ombudsman Association was founded at Islamabad in 1996. It is now eight years old. It has so far held a number of meeting in Pakistan, China including Hong Kong and Macao, Philippines, Japan, South Korea, and Iran. Its present membership has grown to 21from 16 since the years of its inception. AOA Conference is held on biennial basis AOA Conference 2002 was held in Beijing and the next Conference was held in Seoul, South Korea for April 2004. The last meeting of the Board of Directors was held at Macao (SAR) peoples Republic of China in October 2003.Resume of the last meeting of the two Organization is given in the Subsequent pares

Meeting of board of director of the international ombudsman institute held from 3rdOctober 2003 meeting of the board of director of the international, Ombudsman institute (IOI) was held in Canada from 1-3 October 2003. the Hon'ble Wafaqi Mohtasib, Mr. Imtaiz Ahmad sahibzada was invited to participate in the meeting of the Bord Directors .Following important decisions were taken at the meeting.

i. Membership appeals Committee will prepare a report Byelaw amendments, in respect of which offices can or cannot become Institutional members.

ii. IOI priorities Committee Regional Training will deliberate on regional training and founding with the assistance of the regional Vice-president. The Committee will prepare and a document for consideration of the 2004 Board of Directors Meeting.

iii. In Order to clarify articles 6(i) Vi, and 19 of the Bye-Laws regarding the regional representation of an institutional members how is in authority, as ombudsman, on territories which are located in other regions than the region where he is accredited as regional members, the Board made the decisions to allow the right, for its representatives appointed in these territories to Participate in the meeting and activities sponsored by the institute or by the relevant regional constituency. Taking in to account that the institutional members its representatives participate in these meeting and activities as observers.

iv. Mr. Clare Lewis Q. C. was elected as the president of the IOI.

v. The Board agreed to allow the forum of Canadian Ombudsman to use the training manual for 1 year. How ever, it was observed that there should be a requirement that the individuals enrolled in the training session should have some "Investigative responsibilities in their ombudsman position.

International ombudsman man conference June 9-13-2003 at Baku, Azerbaijan

An International Ombudsman Conference was held from June 9-13-2003 in Baku. Republic of Azerbaijan. The commissioner for human rights of Azerbaijan organized the Conference. The main theme of the conference was, role of ombudsman in state based on rule of law.

Meeting of the boar of director of the Asian ombudsman association 20-21 October, 2003 at Macao, people the public of china

Chapter XIII

The annual meeting of the board of director of the Asian ombudsman association was held at Macao, SARC, and people,s Republic of China from 20-21 October 2003. There were 27 delegates from 8th countries, which are member of the board of directors. The Wifaqi Mohtasib as the president of the association addressed the delegate.

The board made the following imported recommendation and decisions:

(i) The board unanimously endorsed the membership of commissioner for human rights of the republic Azerbaijan and provincial Mohtasib (Ombudsman) Balochistan, Pakistan and the commended their cases to the general assembly for ratification during the next session

(ii) A sub-continent of the board was constituted to determine the scope of the proposal and the modalities of its implementations regarding grant of scholarships and financial support in the individual who intend to carry out research / study in the field in ombudsman ship in the member countries

(iii) It was emphasized, that each member of the association should use his good offices to expend the membership of the association

(iv) Member should exchange their respective publications with each other

(v) The AOA website should be linked up with member countries facilitate exchange of information/ views

(vi) Each member of Association should submit a self-contained paper regarding the financial and administrative dispensation under which they are working. The information so submitted would then be integrated to a self-contained paper by the secretariat for information and consideration of the next meeting other board.

(vii) In order to create awareness among general public about effectiveness and usefulness of the office of the ombudsman in the society, it was proposed, that country specific paper on the subject may be submitted of conderatio9n of the board in its next meeting

The AOA secretariat was asked to publish AOA news bulletin on a quarterly basis containing summaries of decisions/recommendations in specific complaints considered important enough for circulations amongst member in addition to any other information deemed significant for sharing with other.

OMBUDSMAN OFFICE (WORLDWIDE)

AFRICA

Botswana ,Burkina Faso, Gabon, Ghana, Lesotho, Madagascar, Malawi, Mauritania, Mauritius,

Namibia, Nigeria , Senegal, Seychelles, South Africa, Swaziland, Sudan, Tanzania, Tunisia, Uganda, Zambia, Zimbabwe

ASIA

Hong Kong, India, Macau, Pakistan, Philippines, South Korea, Sri Lanka, Taiwan, Japan

AUSTRALIA & PACIFIC

Cook Islands, Fiji, New Zealand, Papua, New Guinea, Solomon Islands, Vanuatu, Western Samoa

CARIBBEAN & LATIN AMERICA

Antigua, Barbuda, Argentina, Barbados, Brazil, Colombia, Costa Rica, El Salvador, Guatemala, Guyana, Haiti, Honduras, Jamaica, Mexico, Panama, Paraguay, Peru, Saint Lucia, Trinidad, Tobago Venezuela

EUROPE

Austria, Belgium, Bosnia-Herzegovina, Croatia, Cyprus, Denmark, Germany, Greenland, Hungary, Iceland, Ireland, Israel, Italy, Latvia, Liechtenstein, Lithuania, Macedonia, Malta, Netherlands, Norway, Poland, Portugal, Romania, Russian Federation, Slovenia, Spain, Sweden, Switzerland, United Kingdom, Uzbekistan, European Union

NORTH AMERICA

Canada, United States of America

CHAPTER 14

BIBLIOGRAPHY

Chapter XIV

Chapter XIV

DAVID. W. WILLIAMS
Prectice of the British Ombudsmen and similar bodies.

Donald-C.Rawat-1965
The Ombudsman – Citizen's Defender.

WALTER-GELLHORN
Ombudsman and other: Citizen's Protector in Nine Countries

FRNK.A. STACEY
Ombudsmen Compared

RAJANI RANJAN JHA
Lokayukta-The Indian Ombudsman

FRANK.A. STACEY
The British Ombudsmen

Geoffery Sawer
Ombudsmen

International Handbook of the Ombudsmen
Evolution and Present Function Vol.1

Gerald E.Caiden Aulkes
Administrative Law.

KARL. A. FRIEDMANN
Complaining Comparative aspects of complaint behavior and attitudes towards Complaining

in Canada and British.

LARRY. B. HILL
The Model Ombudsmen-Institutionalizing New Zealand's Democratic Experiment

MARY SENEVIRAINE
Ombudsmen in the Public Sector (Law & Political Change in 1994.

International Handbook of the Ombudsmen
Country Survey-2 Geral E.Caiden (Editor)

MIKAEL HIDAEN
The Ombudsman in Finland –The first fifty Year

RHODA JAMS
Private Ombudsmen and Public Law 1997

ROYGREGORY
Practice and Prospects of the Ombudsman in the United Kingdom 1997

SAM ZOGORIA
The Ombudsman-How Good Governments Handle Citizen's Grievances.

SUBASH CHADRA GUPTA
Ombudsman Perspective.

TIMOTHY.L.FITZHARRIS
The Desirability of a correctional Ombudsman.

Chapter XIV

D.C.M. Yardley
Principles of Administrative Laws.

Utley.T.E
Occasion for Ombudsman

ABRAHAM.H.J.
"Peoples Watchdog Against Abuse of Power"

AIKMAN.C.C.
The New Zealand Ombudsman: XLII Canadian Bar Review. (September, 1964)

ANDERSON S.V.
'The Scandinavian Review (December, 1964)

ANDREN-NILS.
'The Swedish office of Ombudsman'. Municipal Review (1962).

BLOM-COOPER L.J.
'An Ombudsman in Britain?. Public Law (1960)

CHAPMAN-B.
The Ombudsman: "38 Public Administration (London 1960)

CHRISTENSEN.B.
The Danish Ombudsman 109. University of Pennsylvania Law Review

Chapter XIV

DAVIS./A.G.
The Ombudsman in New Zealand, 4-Journal of the International Commission of Jurists (1962 -63)

HURWITZ.S
The Ombudsman (Copenhagen Den Danske Selskeb 1961.

KENT GEORSE
'Watchdog For The Common Man', Rotarian July 1963) Condensed in Reader's Digest (August, 1963)

MARSHALL GEOFFRY
'The New Zealand Parliamentary Commissioner (Ombudsman Act 1962-Public Law (1963)

Swedish Parliamentary
Report for the period July 1990– June–1991 Ombudsman.

Pakistan Wafaqi Mohtasib
Complaint Handing Procedures and (Ombudsman) Instructions Consolidated Circulars No.1,2,3 & 4)

Wafaqi Mohtasib (Ombudsman) Pakistan
Annual Reports 1983 to 2004.

Provincial Ombudsman (Mohtasib) Sindh
Annual Reports 2004.

Provincial Ombudsman (Mohtasib) Azad Jammu &

Kashmir
Annual Reports (1991to 2004).

Provincial Ombudsman (Mohtasib) Punjab
1997- 2004.

THIRD ASIAN OMBUDSMAN CONFERENCE
April 2004

Meeting Report of International Ombudsman Institute held on 1-3 October 2003.

Meeting Report of the Board of Directors of the Asian Ombudsman Association dated 20-21 October 2003.

Bye-laws ratified in November 2000 by the board of Directors of International Ombudsman Institute (IOI).

Meeting Report of Asian Ombudsman dated April 2004.

Miscellaneous

- Muir. E and muir W.(1976) Frans Kafka: the Trial. Martin Secker & Warburg Limited/Octopus Books Limited. London.
- The Ehtasab Act. 1997 (Act IX of 1997) and the National Accountability

ordinance, 1999 (Ordinance XVIII of 1999)

- See generally Klitgarrd. R. (1988) Controlling Corruption, University of California Press, Berkley.
- Ordinance XXXV of 2002.
- Preamble to the Establishment of the Office of Federal Tax Ombudsman Office. 2000.
- Article 10 of the Riksdag Act.
- Parliamentary Commissioner (Ombudsman) Act 1962 (as amended by the Ombudsman Act,1975)
- Parliamentary Commissioner Act. 1967
- See Gwyn B. William (1973). The Brithish PCA: Ombudsman or Ombudsmouse. Journal of Politics February 1973.
- See Select Committee. Minutes of Evidence .5 December 1989 QQ 14-16.
- See First Report from the Select Committee. 1990-91. H.C. 19 December 1990 p. xiii.

Chapter XIV

- See Second Report from the Select Committee.
- 1991-92 (The Implications of the citizens Charter for the Work of the Parliamentary Commissioner for Administration) H.C. 158,5 February 1992,
- Minutes for Evidence. 18 December 1991 .63
- Gregory R. & Pcarson J. (1993)The Parliamentary Ombudsman after twenty five years: Problems and Solutions in Hawke n. Prof. Ed.(1993) The Ombudsman Twenty Five Years On, Cavendish publishing limited. London.
- Establishment of the Office of Ombudsman Sindh Act 1992(Sindh Act No. 1 of 1992).
- The Punjab Office of the Ombudsman Act. 1997 (Punjab Act No. IV of 1997).
- Establishment of the Office of the Federal Tax Ombudsman Ordinance

2000 (Ordinance XXXV) of 2000)

- To clarify the same the Federal tax Ombudsman in Shah-e-Elahi vs. Secretary Revenue Division Islamabad 2002 PTD 1918 outlined his complete interpretation of the provisions of section 9 of the EFTO.

- Sub-section (1) of Section 4 of the Establishment of the Office of the Federal tax Ombudsman Ordinance 2000.
- Defined by sub-section (7) of Section 2 of the Establishment of the Office of the Federal Tax Ombudsman 2003.
- Defined by sub-section (10) of section of the Establishment of the Office of the Federal Tax Ombudsman 2003.
- 1899 AC 99
- 1899 AC 99 at pg. 105-106.
- 1991 SCMR 543 at pg.549
- PLD 1989SC 128 at pg. 134

Chapter XIV

- PLD 1971 SC 205 at pg. 212
- See Dr. Zahid Ahmed Khan vs. Secretary, Revenue Division Islamabad 2002 PTD 2223:

- Business Secretary Technology (Private)Limited vs. Secretary, Revenue Division Islamabad 2002 PTD 1974:
- Iftikhar Ahmad Malik vs. Secretary, Revenue Division, Islamabad 2003 PTD 2307.
- Muhammad Ramzan vs. Secretary Revenue Division 2002 PTD 20307. International Bottlers (Pvt.) Ltd.
- Hyderabad vs. Secretary, Revenue Division Islamabad 2002 PTD 2265.
- Tech Society Limited vs. Secretar, Revenue Division Islamabd 2003 PTD 1498.
- Khyber Spinning Mills Gaddoon vs. Secretary Revenue Division Islamabad 2002 PTD 2646

- Indus Jute Mills Limited Karachi vs. Secretary Revenue Division Islamabad 2002 PTD 2993 at pg. 2795 (1859) 28 L.J.M.C. 213 at pg. 215.
- PLD. 2000 SCC III also Don Basco High School vs. The Assistant Director EOBI PLD 1989 SC 128 at pg.133 PLD 2000 SC 111 at pg. 158
- See Fakir S.Ayazuddin, Paramount Aviation Pvt. Ltd. vs. Commissioner of Income Tax.
- Cpanies-1 Karachi vs. Secretary Revenue Division Central Board of Revenue, Islamabad 2002 PTD 2638:
- Rais Khan , Superintendent Engineer, Central Civil Circle PWD Lahore vs. Secretary Revenue Division Islamabad 2002 PTD 2072 :
- Muhamamd Nazir vs. Secretary Revenue Division Islamabad 2002 PTD 1854: Rkhsana Amjad vs. Secretary, Revenue

Division Islamabad 2002 PTD 2562.

- Nauman Industries , Lahore vs. Secretary, Revenue Division Islamabad 2002 PTD 1450
- PLD 1961 SC 403
- See Generally Graig P.P. (2003) Administrative Law. 5th Edition Thompson ans sweet and Maxwell, at pgs. 4-20 PLD 1987 SC 477 at pg. 453
- Campbell h.(1990)
- Black's Law Dictionary. 6th Edition. West Publishing St. Paul Minnesota at Pg. 1288.
- Hasan vs. Fancy Foundation PLD 1975 SC 1 at Pg. 6:
- Muhammad Haroon vs. The Crown PLD 1951 FC 118 at Pg. 124-125:MNaziruree Brewery Company Ltd. Vs. Pakistan PLD 1972 SC 279 at pg. 290.

Chapter XIV

APPENDIX I

ABOUT AUTHOR

The Author was born at Gojra District Toba Tek Singh, Pakistan.

He did his graduation in B. Com from The University of Punjab. He did his LLB from Bahauddin Zakariya University, Multan and he awarded the degree of LLM from University of Karachi, Karachi. He did advance correspondence course in USUL-AL-FIQH and correspondence course in Islamic law from International Islamic University Islamabad, Pakistan

He took active part in debates during his educational career. He started legal practice in 2000 at Faisalabad. He enrolled as Advocate High Court on 3 March, 2005. He is practicing in the field of Constitutional, Civil, Criminal, Commercial, Corporate, Sale Tax, Income Tax and Banking Laws.

Several time, he appeared before Honourable Federal Tax Ombudsman in different cases. Many of his cases have been approved for reporting in leading Law Digests as well as in Annual reports prepared by his lordship, the Federal Tax Ombudsman, Pakistan. Ample of his articles have been published in reputed Journals and News paper.

APPENDIX I

APPENDIX II

INDEX

A

B

C

D

E

F

G

H

I

J

APPENDIX II

NOTES

NOTES

NOTES

NOTES

www.ingramcontent.com/pod-product-compliance
Lightning Source LLC
LaVergne TN
LVHW090306210926
848480LV00001B/147
* 9 7 8 0 6 1 5 1 4 6 9 2 8 *